Making Money from Renewable Energy
A Guide for Homeowners

Making the Best Use of
Renewable Energy
Incentive Programs

First Edition

Niraj Chandra

Permissions

Feedback

The author welcomes constructive feedback from readers. Please send your comments and suggestions for improvements to the author at:

Niraj_chandra@hotmail.com

The author will consider using this information for the next edition of the book.

Dedications

First and foremost, this book is dedicated to my father, the late Mahesh Chandra, a renowned journalist of his time. He gave me the most precious memories of my childhood – a home filled with books, knowledge, love and laughter.

This book is also dedicated to my brother-in-law Vipin Prasad who first introduced me to the world of Feed-in Tariffs, the inspiration behind much of this book.

I also dedicate this book to my philosophical guru, North America's first environmentalist, Henry David Thoreau of Walden fame. He gave the world this mantra:

"Simplify, Simplify"

I believe in using technology to simplify our lives; used correctly, it can make our lives so much easier. Using renewable energy in the home is a perfect example of this. Henry, wherever you are, I hope you agree with this.

Finally, I dedicate this book to my spiritual guru, Swami Chidvilasananda, who taught me the very essence of good writing with this simple phrase:

"Be clear, be very clear, be crystal clear, be super crystal clear"

Acknowledgements

I want to thank my friend and colleague Subhash Chander, who urged me to write this book, when all I wanted to do was relax in my home. Thank you very much for disturbing the peace.

I must thank my wife Anila for supporting me at every stage of writing this book, right from the time I had this strange idea of trying to change the world we live in by encouraging the use of renewable energy. She has been a source of strength and always brings a much-needed dose of reality to my thoughts.

I also want to thank my niece Mitali Mathur who allowed me the use of her home in Minneapolis for a very creative two weeks, when the foundations of this book were laid.

Also, thanks to my daughter Neha Shah and my son Shavak Chandra for checking the contents of this book and making sure they make some kind of sense to readers.

I extend heartfelt thanks to my friend Harry Jarda for going through every page of this book and making sure it all reads good.

Most of the photographs in this book are the courtesy of the National Renewal Energy Laboratory, The US Department of Energy. Many thanks for making these wonderful pictures available to users.

Disclaimer

Reference to any commercial product or service does not imply, in any way, an endorsement, written or implied, for that product or service. Sometimes, commercial products are referenced in this book, but only by way of illustration. Users must do their own research to select the right product for their specific application.

Design guidelines given in this book are general in nature. They must not be construed in any way as indicating any kind of design recommendations. Again, users must do their own research when designing a system and ensure that they comply with all applicable codes and regulations. The author does not assume any responsibility, written or implied, for any projects that a reader might develop based on the information contained in this book.

Table of Contents

Chapter 1: Getting Started 11
    1.1   Introduction...12
    1.2   Outline of the Book..20
    1.3   Myths about Renewable Energy 21
Chapter 2: The Best Thing since Sliced Bread 27
    2.1   Feed-in Tariffs 28
    2.2   Advantages of FITs..38
    2.3   Drawbacks to FITs..39
    2.4   Crafting FITs That Work 40
    2.5   Applying for Feed-in Tariffs.......................................41
    2.6   RESOP 43
    2.7   Connecting To the Grid 43
    2.8   Net Metering 45
    2.8   Other Incentives..48
Chapter 3: The Energy Market Place..51
    3.1   Know the Energy Marketplace 52
    3.2   Know Your Utility Bill 57
Chapter 4: Plan Your Solar Electric Project 65
    4.1   The Planning and Design Process................................66
    4.2   The Planning Process...69
Chapter 5: Design Your Photovoltaic System 97
    5.1   The Design Phase...98
    5.2   Photovoltaic System Fundamentals 99
    5.3   Solar Energy Fundamentals 107
    5.4   Locating Solar Panels 111
    5.5   Sizing Your Panel 118
    5.6   Panel Mounting Options 123
    5.7   Inverter Selection..125
    5.8   Disconnect Switch Selection.....................................129
    5.9   Wiring Selection 130
    5.10   Other Accessories 134
    5.11   Prepare Schematics 134
    5.12   Prepare Bill of Materials...136
    5.13   Verify all details..137
    5.14   Solar PV Kits 137

Chapter 6: Lining Up Your Permits.................................141
  6.1   The Approval Process.................................142
  6.2   The Building Permit Folks.........................143
  6.3   Getting Past the OPA................................144
  6.4   Satisfying the ESA....................................149
  6.5   Applying for Utility Connection................151
Chapter 7: Installing the Project 153
  7.1   Ordering the Equipment............................154
  7.2   Testing the Equipment 155
  7.3   Installing the Roof- top Panels..................157
  7.4   Installing the electrical equipment.............158
  7.5   Starting the system....................................159
Chapter 8: Other Renewable Energy Projects 161
  8.1   Introduction..162
  8.2   Solar Heating 163
  8.3   Wind Power 169
  8.4   Water Power...173
Chapter 9: The Future of Renewal Energy 177
Chapter10: Useful Resources......................................189
Chapter 11: Glossary of Terms 193
Chapter 12: List of Abbreviations...............................197
Quick Index..199

List of Figures

Figure 1-1:   Feed-in Tariffs

Figure 1-2:   Book Outline

Figure 2-1:   The Feed-in Tariff Process

Figure 4-1:   Planning & Design Process

Figure 5-1:   Grid-Intertie Systems

List of Tables

Table 2-1:   Tariffs throughout the World

Table 2-2:   Connecting to the Utility Grid

Table 3-1:   Anatomy of a Utility Bill

Table 4-1:   Ontario's Feed-in Tariffs

Table 4-2:   North America's Feed-in Tariffs

Table 4-3:   Document Your Plan

Table 5-1:   Recommended Tilt Angles

Table 5-2:   Insolation Data

Table 5-3:   Design Efficiency of Solar Array

Table 5-4:   Solar Panel Sizes & Models

Table 6-1:   The Approval Process

Chapter 1: Getting Started
Contents

1.1   Introduction
1.2   Outline of This Book
1.3   Myths About Renewal Energy

A Large Rooftop Solar Array
Courtesy: National Renewal Energy Research Laboratory, US Department of Energy

1.1 Introduction

What?

Another book on renewable energy?

There are tons of books already written on this topic, you may say, beating this subject to death. Why destroy more rainforests?

But this book is very different. This book will tell you how to *make* money from renewal energy in the very home you live in; others will only tell you how to *spend* more money on renewable energy.

This book *begins* with a discussion of the latest incentives that have made it easier than ever before to make a profit out of renewal energy, such as Canada's Feed-in Tariff program. Other books will preach about the environmental benefits of renewable energy programs and will only incidentally touch upon the incentive programs.

For us, the environmental benefits are a given; they have led to the creation of the incentive programs that we describe. We simply tell you how to reap the maximum benefits from these programs. That way, you can feel good about helping the environment and make some money, too. No other book on the subject will do that for you.

Some of these latest incentives, called Feed-in Tariff (FITs), are not government grants or subsidies. They are self-financing policy instruments where the utilities pay you money, at a very attractive rate, for generating renewal energy. The utilities, in turn, recover the money from their large consumer base. In our opinion, FITs are the best thing since sliced breads and they form much of the inspiration for this book.

The Feed-in Tariff concept originated in the USA but the Europeans were the first to recognize its true potential. Germany introduced Feed-in Tariffs in 1995 and as a result, the country is now a world leader in solar energy use. Feed-in Tariffs were introduced in Spain where they sparked a renewal energy revolution; wind farms are now sprouting like mushrooms all over the Spanish countryside. FITs have now been adopted by at least 47 other countries around the world including Canada and the list keeps growing every year.

The US has been slow in adopting FITs; as a result it has slipped from being a world leader in renewable energy production to going way down the pecking order. There was a time, about two decades back, when the US produced more wind power than any other country in the world but this just isn't true anymore. The US has been overtaken by countries like cloudy Germany, which have more limited wind energy potential; these countries just have better incentive programs.

Ontario, Canada has taken a bold step in this direction by introducing Feed-in Tariff programs patterned after the European model. Following Ontario's lead, some parts of the US, like Vermont, have now taken to FITs. As more policy makers begin to see their benefits, they will, no doubt, be used more and more in the US where it all began.

You, too, can realize the benefits of FITs with the help of this book. We will guide you through the entire process, explaining what FITs are all about. In simple, practical terms, we will help you chose the right project for your home and walk you through the entire process of planning, designing and implementing the project.

This book will explain what permits are required and how to apply for them. It will also tell you how much of the work you can do yourself and when you need to call for help. It will guide you in choosing the right energy consultant or electrical contractor, when you need one. When you need outside help, you need to know exactly what you are looking for and what questions to ask; this book will be your guide.

This book is not written for rocket scientists; you don't have to be an engineer or an architect to understand what is written. You don't even have to be a handyman. Let me confess: I am an engineer but not much of a handyman, as my wife will readily testify. However, I do believe in renewable energy incentives and trust me – this book will show you how to make these incentive programs work for you.

All you need, really, is a strong interest in renewable energy and a desire to make money out of it in your home. This book is not intended for big businesses, either – it is aimed more at the ordinary homeowner who owns a modest home in North America and has limited spending money.

Renewable energy is no longer a fad for dedicated

environmentalists, or a toy for the rich and famous who want to add some "green" credentials to their name while living in huge, energy-guzzling mansions. Just about anybody who owns a home can benefit from this book. The only requirement, really, is that you should live in an area where renewable energy incentive program apply.

And even if you don't have such a program in your area, you can always lobby your local politician for one. With the information contained in this book, you can find a receptive ear wherever you live.

Here is how the Feed-in Tariff program works.

- ❑ You set up a renewal energy project, such as a solar electric photovoltaic system, in your home or community;
- ❑ You get the necessary permits and approvals;
- ❑ You connect to the local utility grid using a "smart" meter which, essentially, measures the flow of power *to* the utility;
- ❑ The utility pays you for renewal energy at an enhanced rate (80cents/KWH in Ontario) which is much higher than the rate at which power is supplied to your home;
- ❑ You are guaranteed this rate for the next twenty years or so to help you recover your investment;
- ❑ The utility, in turn, recovers its costs by spreading them over its very large customer base;
- ❑ The increase in the utility bill for the individual customer is negligible – maybe a just few cents more on the utility bill, which

many customers would not even notice;
❏ You sit back and enjoy the savings.

This process is illustrated in the figure below, for a typical home in Ontario, Canada, where the utility rate is around 15 cents/KWH:

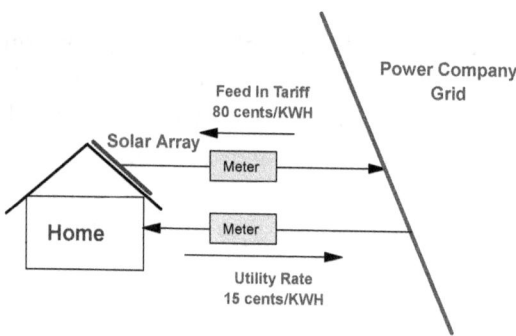

Figure 1-1: Feed-in Tariffs

The Sample Project given below shows how this program can work for you. As you go through this book, you will find that the Sample Project appears again and again, to illustrate the various points being made.

Exercise 1-1:Benefits of Feed-in Tariffs

Sample Project: Located in Ottawa, Ontario

Objective: To explore benefits of a home renewable energy project.

Site Description: Consider that you live in a typical home in a developed neighbourhood of

Ottawa, Canada. It is a three-bedroom house with two south-facing roofs, ensuring good availability of solar energy.

Electricity costs are around 15 cents/KWh for your electricity, considering both fixed and variable charges in the utility bill; the exact rate would vary, depend upon factors such as location, time of use and whether you get electricity directly or from a reseller. You decide to install photovoltaic panels that convert solar energy directly into electricity. What benefits can you expect from this project?

Analysis

You are eligible for incentives under Ontario's Feed-in Tariff program, a part of its Green Energy Act. This program has its highest rates for rooftop solar electricity generation.

If you install solar panels to meet just 10% of your home's electrical consumption, you will be paid at 80 cents/KWH. This is more than five times the price you pay for electricity consumed. Just do the math – five times 10% equals 50%. So you will save 50% of your utility bill.

If you install solar panels to meet 20% of your electricity needs, you will reduce your electricity bill by 100%! In other words, you will get free electricity after making this investment. If you produce even more renewable energy, you will be paid for the electricity you produce at the attractive rate of 80 cents/KWH and you have a profitable business running from right inside your own home!

Results

Installation of solar photovoltaic panels can be very profitable for you.

Before you start setting up a renewable energy project, there are, of course, plenty of other details to be worked out. You need to decide how much you want to invest and what will be the return on the investment. You have to examine the renewable energy potential of your home and decide what type of project is best suited for your home. Then you need to plan your project, work out all the design details, and bring the project to completion. And this is precisely what the rest of this book is all about.

Incentives for renewable energy production have always existed, but they have never been as attractive as they are right now. Before the FITs came along, most states had a very different program, called Net Metering.

With this program, you had to produce enough renewal energy to meet all your electricity needs. Then, if you had some surplus, you could sell it to a utility company and get a credit for the energy supplied – much like a store credit. The utility company never paid you directly – you just got an adjustment to the electricity bill. Net Metering still exists in many parts of North America and we will discuss it in greater detail in the next chapter.

Many states have other incentive programs but most of them are geared towards big business because that is the way that North America works. For the homeowners, there are rebates and tax deductions including the well-known Home Owners' Incentive Program in Canada. Some of these incentives can help you with the capital costs of your equipment but nothing even comes close to the benefits you can get under the Feed-in Tariff program.

This book will tell you more about Feed-in Tariff in the next chapter. It will explain exactly how the program works and point all its advantages and some of its drawbacks. FITs are also known by different names in different parts of the world. They have been called Advanced Energy Tariffs and the Renewable Energy Standard Rate Contract.

In North America, only some states have Feed-In Tariff programs. If you live in Ontario, Canada you are very lucky as this province has one of the most advanced FIT programs in the world. In the US, FITs have been introduced in Vermont, Florida and a handful of other states. However, given the success of the European model it is only a question of time before other parts of North America adopt such programs.

If your state does not have a FIT program, you can always lobby for one by approaching your local politician – after all, it costs the government very little and provides almost unlimited incentives for rapid growth of renewable energy. Using the information given in this book, you will find a receptive ear and you will have made your own little contribution to improving the world you live in.

1.2 Outline of the Book

The contents of this book are outlined in schematic form because a good schematic is worth a thousand words.

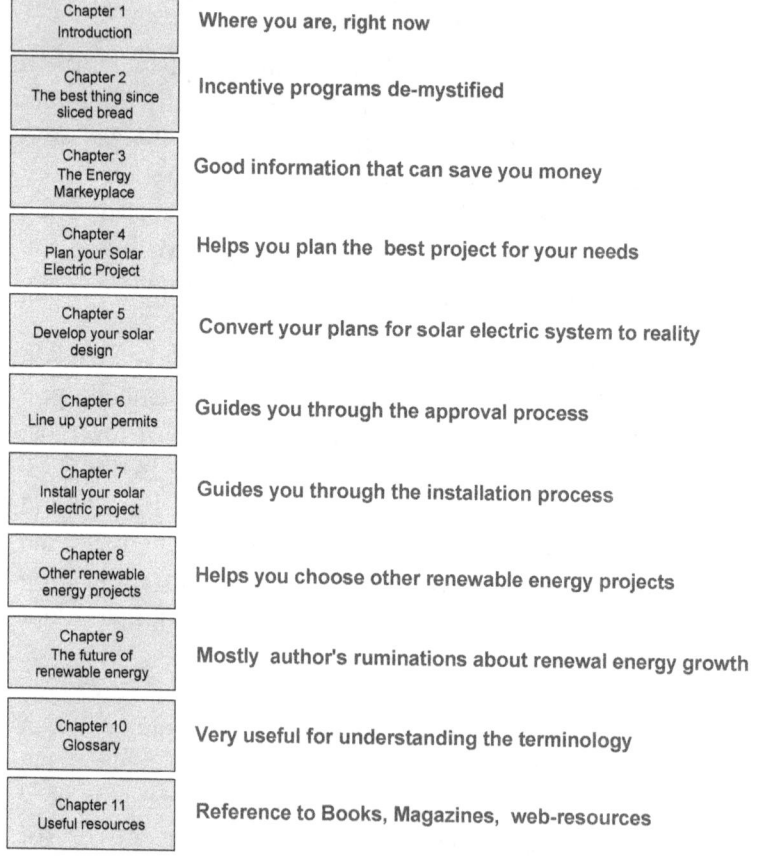

Chapter 1
Introduction
Where you are, right now

Chapter 2
The best thing since sliced bread
Incentive programs de-mystified

Chapter 3
The Energy Markeyplace
Good information that can save you money

Chapter 4
Plan your Solar Electric Project
Helps you plan the best project for your needs

Chapter 5
Develop your solar design
Convert your plans for solar electric system to reality

Chapter 6
Line up your permits
Guides you through the approval process

Chapter 7
Install your solar electric project
Guides you through the installation process

Chapter 8
Other renewable energy projects
Helps you choose other renewable energy projects

Chapter 9
The future of renewable energy
Mostly author's ruminations about renewal energy growth

Chapter 10
Glossary
Very useful for understanding the terminology

Chapter 11
Useful resources
Reference to Books, Magazines, web-resources

Figure 1-2: Book Outline

1.3   Myths about Renewable Energy

Before ending this chapter, let us explore some common myths and misconceptions about renewal energy.

Myth 1: It takes more energy to manufacture photovoltaics than they will ever produce.

Not true. This widely circulated myth has been created by some people who do not support renewable energy.

The energy payback time (EPBT) for a photovoltaic module is one to three years. This means that the energy consumed in producing a photovoltaic panel will be recovered within one to three years of operation according to some estimates. More conservative estimates place the EPBT at three to five years.

Typically, photovoltaic panels last over thirty years. This means that, essentially, they continue to produce electricity long after the energy used in their production has been recovered.

Myth 2: Renewable energy is only for big business

Not true anymore. This was true in the past when government incentive programs   favoured only large companies, thanks to the efforts of powerful lobby groups. This led to the development of large - scale wind farms and solar electricity projects throughout North America.

Today's incentive programs are very different. Feed-in Tariffs – the newest incentives for renewal energy projects – target homeowners, farmers and small businesses. You can make money simply by installing a few solar panels on your roof and connecting to the grid. This book will show you exactly how to do this.

To a large extent, Net Metering programs also target homeowners and small renewable energy producers.

Myth 3: Renewable energy projects require energy storage

Not true at all, unless you want to live off the grid, something we don't recommend in this book. In most cases, the grid will serve as your energy reservoir, giving you electricity when you need it and storing it for you when you don't need it.

So, you don't need storage batteries, anymore, for your next renewable energy project.

Myth 4: Renewable energy projects are expensive

Not true, unless you *want* to spend a lot of money. You can start with a few thousand dollars and invest in some solar photovoltaic panels on your rooftop. You will get a steady return on your investment as the utility company will pay you money at several times the energy supply rate, under the new FIT program.

Windmills may cost a bit more, because you need land, you have to buy wind turbine and you need investment in a tower. But, again, the costs are now within the range of many home or farm owners.

Myth 5: Renewable energy projects require technical expertise

Not true, in general. Some projects do but mostly they don't. Solar PV panels are the easiest to install – just mount them on the roof or in your backyard. The bulk of the wiring is low voltage and easy to do. The high voltage wiring, including the connection to the grid, does require the services of a qualified electrician, for safety reasons.

Wind farms require more expertise to install, but the level of technology is still fairly low. Solar heating systems do not use a high level of technology and a homeowner with good handyman skills should be able to install and maintain them.

Myth 6: Renewal energy projects are heavy maintenance

Not true with today's equipment.

In the past, wind energy projects got a bad reputation, as there were frequent breakdowns and outages. Also, wind was considered an unreliable source of power. However, technology has improved tremendously in the last decade or so. Today's windmills require far less maintenance.

Solar photovoltaic panels are essentially maintenance -free. They use no moving parts so there is nothing to wear out. Once they are installed correctly, they will give you reliable, maintenance-free performance for the next 25 years or so. They don't break down very quickly and you will even forget they exist, until you check your energy savings.

Solar water heating systems do have some maintenance issues. Water can stagnate in the pipeline leading to corrosion and health issues. If the solar heater is not in continuous use, water temperatures can skyrocket and there have been some cases where the solar heating panels have broken down because of the high temperatures.

However, in this book, the focus is on solar PV panels and, to a much smaller extent, on wind energy.

Myth 7: House values decline if you install renewable energy

In fact, the reverse is true, especially with solar photovoltaic panels. Who wouldn't want to live in a house with free electricity? That being said, there is no hard data available right now on how much the home will appreciate, as home renewable energy installations are still not very common.

Myth 8: Renewable energy sources cause noise pollution

This may be true for commercial wind farms where a large number of wind mills have been installed. But again, wind farms are normally installed in remote communities with very little population.

Also, it seems that noise complaints are far less common in Europe where the farmers own their own windmills. The complaints seem to surface more often when ownership is in the hand of large commercial firms, as is often the case in North America.

Solar photovoltaic panels, on the other hand, do not create any kind of noise. They are generally installed in roofs or backyards where they do not even affect the immediate neighbours.

Chapter 2: The Best Thing since Sliced Bread

Contents

2.1   Feed-in Tariffs
2.2   Advantages of Feed-In Tariffs
2.3   Disadvantages of Feed-In-Tariffs
2.4   Crafting a successful FIT program
2.5   RESOP
2.6   Applying for FITs
2.7   Other incentive programs

A Solar Array
Courtesy: National Renewal Energy Laboratory,
US Department of Energy

2.1 Feed-in Tariffs

Sliced bread was a ground breaking invention in its time. It changed bread from being an amorphous mass into a more appetizing product that was easier to use, package, transport and distribute. And of course, it made far better sandwiches! As a result, bread production increased exponentially throughout the world after the introduction of sliced bread.

The Feed-in Tariff (FIT) has done the same thing for renewable energy. It took an amorphous mass of renewable energy programs and provided a very practical form of incentives that are largely self-financing. Wherever FITs have been implemented, renewable energy use has skyrocketed.

This book introduced FITs in the previous chapter. As you might have guessed by now, FITs are a recurring theme in this book. I love them because they bring profits from renewal energy production within the reach of individual homeowners.

The breakthrough concept in FITs is the idea of being self-financing. Renewable energy is paid for at a higher rate and this cost is recovered from other consumers, so that no government subsidy is involved. This is indeed a revolutionary concept, since most other incentive programs depend on government subsidies that are paid for, eventually, by the taxpayer. However, the evolution of FITs occurred in small, baby steps and no one person or group can really claim credit for developing this unique concept.

Even though FITs started in the USA, the subject is still not very well understood in North America. Most people still believe it is some form of government subsidy to encourage the use of renewal energy. This is certainly not true today, even though the program did begin life as a way of subsidizing renewable energy.

Initially, the basic idea was that renewable energy producers should be able to connect to the grid and get paid for the energy that they produced. The utilities were asked by the regulators to set a price for renewable energy at a little less than the cost of conventional electricity. This was called the "avoidance cost" of renewable energy.

Later, some people realized that renewal energy producers should be paid at a higher rate than for conventional energy, because of the considerable environmental benefits that accrue from renewal energy. The "Aha" moment came when somebody, somewhere, realized that the additional cost could simply be passed on to the existing customers. If the customer base was large enough, the effect on each customer would be very small. With the inclusion of this additional step, the process became largely self-financing.

Here is a timeline of how this evolution took place:

1980s	Feed-in Tariff first introduced in California, USA, under the name of Standard Offer Contract. At this stage the idea was simply to allow renewable energy producers to connect to the utility power grid. This was done at the behest of a powerful farmer's

	lobby that had access to a number of disused hydroelectric plants in rural California. The producers were to be paid a fixed rate per KWH, guaranteed for the duration of a ten-year contract. The rate was determined by calculating the cost of energy from a conventional source for the same amount of power – i.e. the avoidance cost. There was no premium price paid for renewal energy.
1984	No new contracts were offered after this year, as energy prices dropped worldwide and the government did not want to spend more money on the program. However, contracts already in force were honoured, leading to a boom in wind energy production in California for the next two decades.
1991	Germany developed regulations for feeding power into the grid from renewable energy sources, introducing the phrase "Feed-in Tariff". The tariff was fixed at 80-90% of the retail electricity rate. Some people suggested that the FIT should be greater than avoidance costs because of environmental benefits. In fact, they suggested that there was no need to link the tariff to the market rate for conventional power. The concept of delinking marked the beginning of FITs as we know them now.
2000	Germany introduced the Renewable Energy

	Sources Act that gave preference to electricity from renewable sources.
	This Act established the basic principle that tariffs should be based on the cost of generation from each technology plus a reasonable profit and they would be guaranteed for twenty years. Thus, the tariff should be different for each type of technology.
	This came to be known as the Advanced Renewable Tariff; for the first time there was a differentiation in the tariff payments by type of renewable energy source.
2000-2004	Germany found that its initial FIT program was not very successful. The tariffs had been set too low and did not attract enough renewable energy generation.
	Hence, it experimented with various tariff structures until it found a structure that worked. The highest tariff was set at the equivalent of 40 cents (US)/KWH. This was about four times the wholesale cost of electricity. Utilities were allowed to recover the FIT costs from other customers.
2004	In its latest revision to the FIT program, Germany increased the tariff for solar PV was increased to 0.57 Euros/KWH, approximately 0.75 US $/KWH.
2006	Ontario, Canada introduced its Renewable Energy Standard Offer Program (RESOP), which is similar to a Feed In Tariff in many

	ways. A guaranteed price for renewable energy was paid over a 20-year contract period. There were only two offers: one for solar photovoltaic panels and another for all other renewable energy sources. The maximum price paid was 42 cents/KWH for solar photovoltaic panels. There was no further differentiation based on the type of technology, so it was not really a full-blown FIT program. The program enjoyed modest success, as many found that the tariffs were not attractive enough. Ontario also offered a Net Metering program.
2008	California, USA, enacted the Feed-in Tariff law
2009	Ontario introduced new tariffs for renewable sources of generation under the Ontario Green Energy and Green Economy Act. The tariffs are differentiated by technology, size, and application. The highest tariff is $0.82 CAD/kWh for residential rooftop solar PVs, one of the highest rates in the world.
May 2009	Vermont enacts feed in tariff law with a structure closely resembling Ontario's tariffs. However, the maximum tariff is only 0.30 $(US)/KWH for solar energy; wind energy tariffs start at 0.12$(US)/KWH
2009	Gainesville, Florida enacts FITs.
2009	11 other legislatures in the US consider FITs

This brief history should provide some understanding of how FITs came into being. However, you are probably still wondering how these tariffs really work out in practice.

Wikipedia explains the process in this way:

"FiT is a revenue-neutral way of making the installation of renewable energy more appealing. The electricity that is generated is bought by the utility at above market prices. For example, if the retail price of electricity is 10¢/kWh then the rate for green power might be 40¢/kWh. The difference is spread over all of the customers of the utility. For example, if $100,000 worth of green power is bought in a year by a utility that has 1,000,000 customers, then each of those customers will have 10¢ added on to their bill annually."

The key points to note in this definition are:

1. FITs are revenue-neutral. The way FITs have evolved, they do not cost anything to the utility, other than purely administrative expenses.
2. FITs offer above-market prices. Under FITs, the utility buys electricity from the renewable energy producer an enhanced rate – in some cases eight or ten times higher than the rate of electricity supply.
3. The difference is spread out over all customers. The remaining customer base pays the price for the renewal energy.
4. $100,000 worth of green power costs just 10 cents/customer, if there are 1,000,000 customers. The example clearly indicates that the impact on the individual customer's bill is so

small as to be negligible.

The FIT process is summarized below:

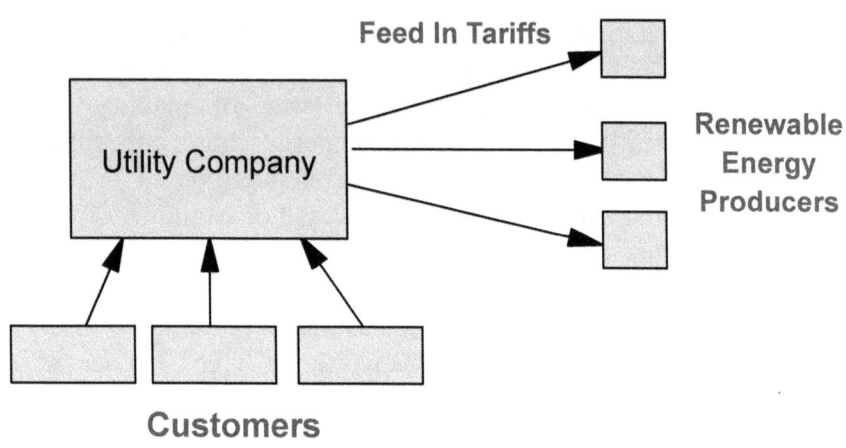

Figure 2-1: The Feed-in Tariff process

The FIT concept works because it is completely revenue-neutral. The tax payer does not have to shell out the big bucks for a complex program. With FITs, the utility pays a premium rate for renewal energy; the cost is spread out over the utilities' customer base.

If the customer base is large enough –as is generally the case- the cost per customer turns out to be very small. In effect, the program is funded by users of electricity, as opposed to other government subsidies where the taxpayer ends up footing the bill. Of course, the government does provide oversight; normally, arms-length government agencies like the Ontario Power Authority set-up and manage these programs.

A key component of the FIT program is a long-term contract between the energy producer and the utility company. Generally the contract is for 20 years; some utility companies offer shorter contracts of 15 years or less. The contract ensures that the renewable energy producer is paid a fixed rate for the energy produced, guaranteeing a certain minimum return on the investment.

Sometimes, there is a de-escalation clause built into the contract; this ensures that, after fifteen years or so, the tariff starts declining. This clause simply recognises the fact that once the renewal energy project has paid for itself, it does not need the same level of incentives as before.

Yet another important component of the FIT program is the use of   dual metering. An FIT system uses two meters: a conventional meter to measure the consumption of electricity supplied to the customer and another "smart" meter that measure the electricity supplied to the grid. The utility company is responsible for providing both of these meters.

Effectively, there are two systems at work: the conventional electricity supply and, the renewable energy system. There are several different ways of inter-connecting the two systems and this will be discussed in more detail in Chapter 4, where we talk about planning the renewable energy project.

In North America, the FIT concept has been known by many other names: Electricity Feed Laws, Advanced Renewable Tariffs (ARTs), Renewable Tariffs, Production Incentives, and more recently,

Renewable Energy Payments.

However, it is more appropriate to think of the FIT as a policy instrument set up to encourage the growth of renewal energy. Viewed in that light, it is a very effective instrument. Other policy instruments that have been used include Net Metering and subsidies for "green" energy production, which have generally gone to large energy producers. FITs on the other hand, help the small producer and lead to a much more rapid growth in renewable energy production.

Purists often object to FIT programs on the grounds that they are not equitable. They claim that the cost of renewable energy production is being passed on customers who do not produce renewable energy. Why should they have to bear these costs? However, the actual impact on individual customers is very small, as shown by the Wikipedia example. In any case, utilities have never hesitated in passing on other costs to their customers.
Just take a look at your utility bill –the company charges you for electricity consumed plus it tacks on distribution charges and even debt retirement charges.

The question really is: should the electricity consumers subsidize "green" power generation or, should the taxpayer have to do this through a government-run program that they can never understand?

To me, it seems far more equitable to let the electricity consumers subsidize the program; why should all taxpayers be on the hook? Also, which is better - a transparent FIT program, or, a subsidy program hidden behind layers of bureaucracy?

Few people realize that power generation has almost always been subsidized in one form or another. There have always been tax breaks and special grants given to the energy companies. In the US, the energy lobby has always been powerful and it has made sure that the big energy producers get their share of government benefits. In every case, it is the taxpayer who ends up footing the bill and most of the time the taxpayer does not even know where the money is going. It makes far more sense to use a transparent device such as an FIT program that offers clarity on where the money is coming from and where it is going.

Here is a comparison of Ontario's FIT structure with other parts of the world.

Table 2-1: Tariffs throughout the World			
Country	Application	Tariff, In Euro/KWH	Tariff, In CAN $/KWH
Italy	Rooftop Solar	.54	0.85
South Korea	Rooftop Solar	.57	.89
France		.6	.946
Ontario, Canada	Rooftop Solar		.80
Germany	Rooftop Solar	.468	.74
Austria	<5KW	.46	.72

Source: http://www.wind-works.org

Of course, any incentive program needs revision from time to time. If the current program in Ontario leads to a massive boom in renewable energy production, the tariffs may well be revised downwards after a few years. Some countries like Germany even have a tariff reduction clause built into some of their FIT programs.

We believe the best time to profit from Canada's program is right now, before the field gets too crowded. Prices of solar photovoltaic panels and wind turbines are also subject to change. There has been a steady downwards trend for the last few years due to increased production.

However, there is no guarantee that this downward trend will continue. If worldwide production of photovoltaic grade silicon declines, there could well be a price increase in the years to come.

2.2   Advantages of FITs

To summarize, Feed-in Tariff programs offer the following advantages:

- ✓ They apply equally to small and large producers of renewable energy;
- ✓ The system is largely self-financing;
- ✓ Administrative costs are low, as there is not much to administer;
- ✓ Incentives are differentiated by the type of technology, so that the payback/rate of return is kept about the same for each type of technology;

✓ For the renewable energy producer, there is a guaranteed return on investment for fixed time period which is more than adequate to pay for the cost of the equipment;

✓ The program is very simple and transparent;

✓ FIT contracts are transferable to the next owner of the home; hence FITs should have a positive impact on home prices

✓ FITs have a successful track record throughout the world, especially in Germany, Spain and France.

2.3 Drawbacks to FITs

Are there any drawbacks to FIT programs? You bet there are – there is no such thing as a perfect system. But the drawbacks are far less numerous than with other incentive schemes.

Here are some objections that have been raised against FITs:

✓ Purists may say there is no need for an incentive program. Why can renewable energy programs not stand on their own merits? Again, the historical record shows that power generation projects have always been given subsidized in one form or another. Very often, it is a hidden subsidy; the taxpayer still pays but is generally kept ignorant of what is going on.

✓ The system will work fine as long as the number of renewable energy producers is small, as has always been the case so far. The system would run into problems if too many people switched to producing renewable energy as the costs to the average customer may increase. This hasn't happened yet.

✓ There may be tax implications, as some authorities may treat payments from the utilities as taxable. Setting up a separate business entity can reduce the taxable amount so that expenses can be deducted; also the rules for depreciation will apply towards capital costs.

✓ The tariff is set somewhat artificially; an agency such as the Ontario Power Authority has to do its homework correctly to come up with the tariff rates; even then, adjustments may be required because the market keeps changing.

2.4 Crafting FITs That Work

Getting the FIT program to work properly is not all that easy; no country or state seems to have got it right the first time around. If the tariff is kept too low, there is not enough incentive for the renewable energy producer. If the tariff is kept too high, the scheme may prove too attractive and stimulate too much activity in the field, pushing up the costs for other consumers.

Also, the tariff has to be just right for each type of renewable energy source; there is no one size that fits all sources. Solar photovoltaic panels require a bigger capital investment than windmills for each unit of power generated.

Hence you cannot have the same FIT rate for the two types of renewal energy. Ideally, the rate should be crafted such that the rate of return is the same for each type of renewable energy source.

Due to the complexity of this task, the FIT program is generally is developed by an independent body such as the Ontario Power Authority (OPA), an arms-length agency of the Ontario government.

Typically, the OPA spends years in developing a program; inputs are sought from all kinds of interest groups. It goes through multiple levels of public consultation before it is enacted into law. After seeing the market response, the system is fine tuned until we get a program that works.

The OPA will revise the FIT program every two years or so, allowing it to adjust the tariffs from time to time. Thus there is no guarantee that today's rates will be valid two years down the road. However, existing contracts that the OPA has already signed will be honoured. The historical record also shows that agencies like the OPA can stop receiving applications at any time, if there is an application overload.

2.5 Applying for Feed-in Tariffs

The Ontario Power Authority has simplified the application process as much as possible. If you install less than 10KW capacity, you don't even have to give a security deposit. These are called microFIT projects.

Most home projects will be less than 10KW, unless you set up a large project for the entire community! The key elements of the OPA rules for small projects (less than 5MW) are summarized below:

- ✓ Your project must have a local content of at least 40%. In most cases, this requirement is easily met because even the Consultancy expenses and installation costs are eligible, if the businesses are in Ontario. Currently, there are not too many suppliers of solar photovoltaic panels in Ontario.
- ✓ You can apply under your own name or, under the name of a business you decide to set up
- ✓ You can also apply for a community project
- ✓ You don't even have to buy the equipment you need; leasing arrangements are acceptable
- ✓ Project must use one of the following technologies: solar photovoltaic, wind, waterpower, landfill gas, biomass or biogas
- ✓ Solar heating projects are excluded as they do not generate electricity
- ✓ Projects must not be part of an existing contract with the OPA, such as RESOP
- ✓ You must sign a long-term agreement with the utility company, after approval of your application. This is called the "connection agreement".

The approval process is described in detail in Chapter 6 where the other approvals required for renewable energy project are also discussed.

Table 2-2: Connecting to the utility grid		
Type of Connection	**Advantages**	**Disadvantages**
Option 1: Series connection	Lower costs, easier installation	If the customer is disconnected from the grid, the renewable energy project will be disconnected.
Option 2:Parallel connection	FIT payment is independent of customer's grid connection	Higher costs; installation requires temporary disconnection from grid
Option 3: Direct	FIT payment is independent of customer's grid connection	Requires separate transformer for renewable energy source; highest costs

In most cases, Option 1 is preferred as it is simple and cost effective, unless you have a good reason to go with Option 2 or Option 3.

2.8 Net Metering

Before the advent of Feed-in Tariffs, Net Metering was widely used throughout North America; it is still in use in many provinces and states. Ontario offers both Net Metering and Feed-in Tariff programs. In Ontario, you can also transition from a Net Metering program to a FIT.

Net Metering works by using a single meter connection that can measure electricity flow in both directions. The meter spins backwards when renewable energy is being generated; it moves forward when electricity is being supplied. Thus, the utility bill is automatically adjusted for the amount of renewable energy that is supplied to the grid.

This form of metering has the advantage of simplicity; in most cases, the existing meter can be used. Also, if the amount of renewable energy produced exceeds the consumption of electricity in the home, the surplus is recorded by the utility as a green credit. This can be used just like a store credit, against future purchases of electricity. See Figure below.

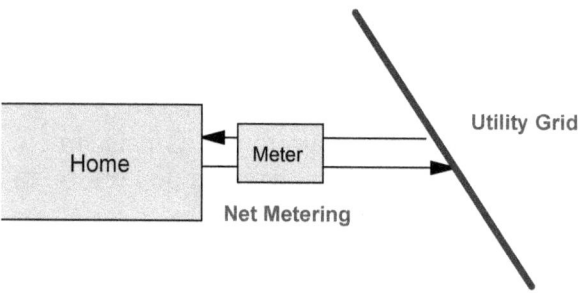

Figure 2-2: Net Metering

Net metering works well in some specific circumstances. For example, a homeowner may produce more electricity than is consumed during the hours of peak sunlight. This will result in a green credit that can be used during the evening when there is no sunlight.

The other big advantage of Net Metering is that the program is easy to administer; there is not much to keep track of.

However, Net Metering does not provide any real incentive for production of renewable energy as payment is only at the market rate for electricity. In most cases, this is not a very attractive rate – certainly not enough to justify setting up an expensive renewable energy project.

With Net Metering, the utility company never pays you real money; it only gives you credits that you can use to offset your energy purchases. In some schemes, the green credits expire annually.

The system is not quite   as effective as FITs. In Net Metering schemes, you get, at best, a reduction in your electricity bill based on current prices. In an FIT scheme, you are paid several times the going rate for supply of electricity.

Just do the math.

Electricity is typically sold at about 15 cents/KWH in Ontario, when you add up all the costs. The FIT for a solar rooftop PV panel will fetch you about five times this rate. So, if you install solar panels to meet 10% of your electricity needs, you get back 50% and you have to pay only 50% of your electricity bill. If you produce more renewable energy, you are riding the gravy train. If you are on Net Metering, you don't make any money –you just spend on the renewal energy project and save some money on the utility bill.

Provinces that offer Net Metering in Canada include British Columbia, Nova Scotia, Ontario and Saskatchewan. In Ontario, you can convert from Net Metering to a FIT program.

The Database of Incentive Programs offers a complete listing of both Net Metering and FIT programs in the US. This site is very comprehensive and offers a wealth of useful information. Check it out at:

http://www.dsireusa.org/

2.8   *Other Incentives*

You might qualify for other incentives for your renewable energy project, depending upon where you live. For example, most homeowners in Canada are eligible for the Home Renovation Tax Credit.

There may be other programs where the government gives you an outright subsidy based on your renewable energy production capacity.

There are also incentive programs for commercial renewal energy production. Normally, only large companies are able to benefit from these schemes. The State of California introduced several programs like this, making this State the US leader in solar energy at one time.
Incentive programs like this have spawned the growth of large wind farms in many parts of US and

Canada. Drive down to upstate New York and you will see hundreds of wind farms in many remote-farming communities owned by large renewal energy developers. Sometimes, these projects are very beneficial as they boost the economy of many remote-farming areas.

Some provinces offer rebates for solar hot water systems. For example, Nova Scotia offers a 10% rebate towards installation of these systems. See the web site:

http://www.ecologyaction.ca/content/incentive-programs

 You could also get a grant for you solar hot water system under the ecoEnergy retrofit program. Check out the site at:

http://oee.nrcan.gc.ca/residential/personal/retrofit-homes/retrofit-qualify-grant.cfm?attr=4#list

Chapter 3: The Energy Market Place

Contents

3.1   Know the Energy Marketplace
3.2   Know Your Utility Bill

A Wind Farm
Courtesy: National Renewal Energy Laboratory, US Department of Energy

3.1 Know the Energy Marketplace

Before you even begin planning your renewable energy project, you must have at least a rudimentary idea of how the energy marketplace works. Be prepared for surprises – the energy marketplace is far more complex than what most people can even imagine. There are hundreds of players in this market place, playing out dozens of roles.

There was a time, not too long ago, when there was just one company who produced, distributed and billed you for the energy that you consumed. If you had a problem, you approached this company for resolution. This just does not happen any more.

So, welcome to the bizarre world of energy deregulation.

In the interests of increasing competition, the government has deregulated the industry. So we now have a larger number of players who monopolize little bits of the market place. Deregulation has created such a maze of producers, regulators, distributors and re-sellers that is enough to confuse any consumer. Sometimes, it seems that the energy industry thrives on complexity that helps it generate more profits.

There are many who believe that deregulation has brought large benefits to the marketplace. They point out that energy prices in North America have stayed almost constant after de-regulation. In fact, with such a competitive marketplace, North America has some of the lowest energy prices in the world.

In North America, the main sources of energy used by homeowners are electricity and natural gas. In most homes, natural gas is used for heating; electricity is used for most other purposes including cooking, lighting and running different appliances. There are, of course, exceptions to this rule; some homes use natural gas for cooking while many older homes still use electric heat. However, for the majority of homes, energy costs are roughly distributed evenly between natural gas and electricity.

In this book, attention is focussed largely on renewable energy incentive programs such as Feed-in Tariff. These incentives apply mostly to electricity; hence in this chapter, only the electricity marketplace is described. The natural gas marketplace is equally complex but that is another subject for another book.

Here is a brief snapshot of the major players in the electricity marketplace. Note that this picture barely scratches the surface but if you are interested you can always find out more – just go to some of the Internet resources listed in Chapter 10.

Also, much of the information given below is based on the Ontario marketplace, simply because the author happens to live in Ontario. Hopefully, other provinces have a similar structure so most of the information should be useful to people living elsewhere. In any case, the purpose of this section is only to give you a little taste of what the energy marketplace looks like and how it would impact your renewable energy project. It is, by no means, a comprehensive listing on the subject. Now meet the key players in the Ontario marketplace:

The Regulators

These are the folks –mostly government agencies – that regulate the power generation system in your province.

In Ontario, the **Ministry of Energy & Infrastructure** sets the legal and policy framework that governs the energy sector.

The Ontario Energy Board implements this policy framework. It also sets the maximum rates that can be charged for supply of power. However, as explained further below, there are ways around the rules and providers can add other charges to your bill.

The Planners

These folks plan ahead – sometimes as much as the next twenty-five years – to make sure the provinces energy needs are met for a long, long time. It is really good to have them around.

The **Ontario Power Authority** is an arms-length agency reporting to the Ontario Government. Among other things, this agency is responsible for developing long-term plans for generation of electric power. It developed the RESOP plan and the Net Metering system. It has developed the plans for Feed -In Tariffs that form the basis for much of this book.

The OPA listens carefully to various interest groups and has extensive public consultations before finalizing a policy. It is also big on developing energy conservation programs.

The OPA gets direction from Ontario's Minister of Energy.

The Generators

These companies actually produce the power that you get. There used to be just one of them but now there are many. This happened in the early 90s when the monolithic Ontario Hydro was broken up into a number of smaller players by government decree, in an effort to bring in more competition into the business.

The largest of these entities is **Ontario Power Generation** that produces 70% of the provinces' electricity. Much of it comes from nuclear energy but there are also hydroelectric plants and coal-based power plants throughout the state.

The Transmitters

Once the electricity is produced, electricity travels across the province over high voltage transmission lines that form part of the national power grid.

And guess what? Other companies own the transmission lines. These companies supply the power into local distribution system, such as Hydro Ottawa. Step-down transformers reduce the transmission voltage to a level fit for distribution to the customer.

The Distributors

They distribute the power locally, over low-voltage distribution lines. You probably know these companies as your local utilities, such as Hydro Ottawa in Ottawa. There are scores of these companies throughout the province. Your utility bill is generated by one of these companies. In a way, these companies still have their little monopolies, because only one company owns the distribution lines in any one area. So, you as the consumer, are totally dependent on your local utility company.

These companies do not, however, own the power that flows through their distribution system. This brings us to the next group of players in the marketplace, the ones who sometimes give the consumers the most trouble.

The Energy Resellers

You might have seen some of their representatives at your door, trying to seduce you into buying a long- term fixed price contract. They buy energy from the producers and re-sell it to the consumer.

There is not too much money to be made by simply buying energy and selling it to the consumer – the margins are razor-thin. So the resellers try to beat the odds by selling you their long-term contracts. Their sales pitch is simple: energy prices fluctuate, so if you lock-in your prices for five years you get peace of mind. It generally works the other way around – it is the resellers who get peace of mind and end up making the big bucks.

The Independent Electricity System Operators

These good folks provide a wonderful service by balancing the supply and demand for electricity at any given time and then directing its flow along the provinces transmission lines. These are not-for-profit organizations, governed by a Board of Directors appointed by the local government.

Every five minutes, the IESO forecasts consumption throughout the province and collects the best offers from generators to provide the required amount of electricity. This allows customers to see prices fluctuate based on supply and demand. As a result, they can shift consumption away from peaks in demand to times when the price is lower.

The IESO is also responsible for emergency preparedness in the province's electricity system.

3.2 Know Your Utility Bill

Utility companies thrive on complexity, just like the rest of the energy marketplace. Your utility bill is a perfect example –there must be a whole department at work, trying to figure out how to add more complexities to it every day. As a result, most customers don't even look at the details on the bill – they just pay it.

The utility bill, does, however, contain a lot of useful information and is definitely worth a closer look. This could even save you a lot of money if it helps you find out where you are being ripped off.

If you examine your bill, you'll find you are paying much more than just the basic electricity rate. This rate, in cents/KWH is just one line item on the bill. There are other line items for distribution charges, debt servicing and much, much more.

The basic electricity rate is regulated by the Ontario Energy Board and shown on the Board's web site. At the time of writing, the rate is in the range of 6-8 cents/KWh; it varies a little based on usage and the time of day. It does change from time to time so it could be totally different when you get around to reading this book. Just check out the latest numbers at the web site:

http://www.oeb.gov.on.ca/OEB/Industry+Relations/
OEB+Key+Initiatives/Regulated+Price+Plan

However, the utility companies have ways to legally charge you much more than the Energy Board rate.

This is how it works.

The Energy Board only regulates how much the utility can charge per KWH i.e. for your electricity consumption. In addition, the utility is allowed to levy electricity distribution charges, regulatory charges and even debt servicing charges.

Also, if you get your electricity from a reseller, you pay the reseller's charges that could be much higher than the Electricity Board rate. If you have a contract with the reseller, you have already agreed to pay the higher rate. In other words, you can get ripped off really badly if you are not a savvy customer.

When I looked at my own utility bill and added up all the different charges, I found I was paying closer to 17 cents/KWh. This final total was not shown on the bill; I had to calculate it using a spreadsheet.

Another element of complexity is the billing cycle itself. For some strange reason, the bill does not follow a monthly cycle – it is more likely to be a bi-monthly cycle. Meter reading follows its own cycle, hence the electricity consumption has to be adjusted to match the billing cycle –this is called the "adjusted" consumption for the billing period.

Most of the time, you can save money simply by studying your utility bill carefully and by making a few telephone calls. When I looked at my own bill in some detail, I found there was a long-term contract with an energy reseller that I wasn't even aware of. Apparently, the reseller had visited our home a few years ago and persuaded my wife to sign a five-year contract to guard against rising electricity prices.

Guess what? The electricity prices did not rise, and four years later I was paying 30% more than the market rate for my electricity. I called the reseller and threatened to cancel the contract; I immediately got a better offer at a 30% lower price.

This was, by no means, the end of the matter. My bill still showed a Provincial Benefit charge that was inexplicable. I called the utility company again and was finally told that this item covered the overhead associated with processing the resellers' charges.

To help you out with this process, here is a quick primer on how your utility bill is set-up. We have used a sample bill from Ottawa Hydro as an example; please allow for regional differences.

Table 3-1: Anatomy of a Utility Bill	
Item	**Description**
Billing Period:	Bi-monthly, in many cases
Account History	Electricity consumption, in KWh, for last 12 months.
Electricity Consumption	Electricity consumption, in KWh, for billing period
Adjusted Electricity Consumption	Electricity consumption adjusted for meter reading cycle
Total bill amount	In dollars
Itemized Break down of bill	Stuff that makes the bill harder to decode
1. OES Energy Charge 2. Provincial Benefit 3. Delivery charges 4. Regulatory Charge 5. GST	
Name of electricity provider	This is the energy reseller who convinces people to sign a long-term contract

You should now be able to get the following information from your utility bill:

1. Electricity rate in $/KWH for month. To get this figure, simply divide your KWh reading by the total dollar amount of the bill. This will give you the charge out rate for a given billing period. It might vary a little from one billing period to another.

   Electricity rate = KWh/(Dollar value of bill)

2. Total electricity consumption for each month; this again, varies from month to month. If you run the air- conditioning a lot, the consumption should peak during July and August. If you use electricity for heating, the winter months may show peak consumption.

3. The average monthly consumption of electricity, in KWh/month. Just take the total of one years' consumption and divide by twelve.

4. The average monthly electricity rate, in $/KWh.

Factoid: The average home in North America uses 936 KWh of power per month (Source: Wikianswers.com).

Once you know the monthly power consumption, you can calculate your average connected load. This is simply the average rate at which you draw power, in KW.

To calculate this number, use the average number of days in a month i.e. 30.4 days divided by 24 hours per day.

Average Connected Load = Average monthly electricity consumption/30.4/24.

Exercise 3-1: Anatomy of a Utility Bill

Sample Project: Located in Ottawa, Ontario
Objective: To analyze the utility bill

Analysis
The electricity in this home is supplied by Hydro Ottawa. The utility bill yields the following information:

| Billing Period: | 60 days (April 6, 2009 to June 6, 2009) |
| Account History: | This section shows meter readings from June 2008 to June 2009. |

Reading date	KWh	Days	KWh/day
2009-06-05	690	60	11.51
2009-04-06	750	59	12.72
2009-02-06	1006	62	16.23
2008-12-06	896	59	15.2
2008-10-08	713	62	11.51
2008-08-07	916	63	14.54
2008-06-05	686	59	11.64

Electricity Consumption	
For billing period	668 KWh
Adjusted Consumption	691 KWh
Total Bill Amount	$152.30
Breakdown of bill:	
OES Energy Charge	$71.50
GST	$3.57

For 24 days

Provincial Benefit	$9.96
Delivery	$15.59
Regulatory Charge	$1.71
Debt Retirement Charge	$1.85
GST	$1.44

For 36 days

Provincial Benefit	$14.50
Delivery	$24.86
Regulatory Charge	$2.68
Debt Retirement Charge	$2.78
GST	$2.25
Electricity provided by Savings(OES) L.P.	Ontario Energy

Results

Total Cost/KWH: $152.30/690.97 = $0.22 /KWH
OES Energy Charge/KWH: $0.10 cents/KWh
Highest Monthly Consumption:1006/2 = 503 KWh
Lowest Monthly Consumption:686/2 = 343 KWh
Ave. Monthly Consumption:(Sum)/12=414 KWh
Annual Consumption   4971 KWh
Consumption/day   4971/365 = 13.6 KWH/day
Consumption/hour   13.6/24 = 0.57 KW
Hence the average load is 0.57 KW for this home

Chapter 4: Plan Your Solar Electric Project

Contents

4.1   The Planning and Design Process
4.2   Plan Your Solar Electric Project

Roof-mounted Solar Panels
Courtesy: National Renewal Energy Laboratory, US Department of Energy

4.1 The Planning and Design Process

The planning design process followed in this book is much like project planning in the business world. The following steps are involved:

1. Plan your project
2. Develop the Design
3. Get Approvals
4. Install the Project

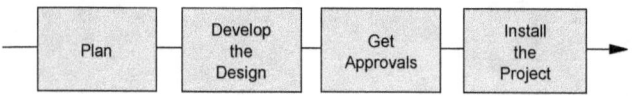

Figure 4-1: The Planning and Design Process

Using a systematic process helps in getting the project off the ground very quickly; it also keeps costs under control as you move from a ballpark estimate during the *planning* stage to more accurate numbers during the *development of the design* stage. Then you seek *approvals* with the authorities for your renewable energy system.

If you have followed this systematic process, *installing the project* will be a piece of cake. Then you need to *get more approvals, connect to the grid* and the project is done.

These phases are described in more detail as follows.

Phase 1: Plan your project

During this stage, you collect background information about renewable energy and define exactly what you want to do. You get ballpark figure for the cost of the project, the time it takes and calculate the approximate return on the investment. You may even decide to opt out of the project or do it in two or three stages, depending upon your budget.

This book should give you most of the information required to complete this stage. Additional sources of information, including web sites are listed in Chapter 11. You should not need any outside consultation during the planning stage.

However, you may not have enough information to file for approvals with various agencies as some of them might want to look at a fully developed design. This leads to the next stage.

Phase 2: Development of the Design

During this stage, you build upon the work done in planning and develop a much more detailed design of the layout of the renewable energy system. You don't get into component design – that is the job of the manufacturer. However, you study the site conditions and do some simple calculations to help you decide exactly what components you need for your project. Then, you prepare schematics and, perhaps, wiring diagrams. You might need to work with an electrician to get all the details right. Also, you will need to prepare a Materials List and also list the specifications for each item.

Phase 3: Getting Approvals

Once your design is complete, you can apply for approvals from various authorities. At the very least, you will need approval from the Ontario Power Authority, if your project is in Ontario, and from your local utility. Approval from municipal authorities may also be required. For wind energy projects, environmental clearances may also be needed.

Phase 4: Install the project

Now we are coming to the good stuff –the installation phase. Now you buy all the needed equipment and test each component to make sure it works correctly. This is the real fun part of the project, when everything starts coming together. This is when you learn the most about the system – when you test everything out to make sure it works exactly as intended.

After component testing is complete, the equipment has to be installed in the correct locations. For your first project we strongly recommend calling in a professional installer, especially if panels are being installed on the roof.

Note: Rooftop panel installation and wiring is dangerous work and we don't recommend that you do it your self.

You will also need the services of a certified electrician to do the final wiring. Again, you cannot do the final wiring yourself, unless you happen to be an expert electrician. The wiring has to meet professional standards as the Electrical Safety Authority will inspect it. You cannot connect to the grid until the renewable energy system passes all safety inspections.

Once everything has been installed correctly, the Electrical Safety Authority will inspect the system and once they give their go ahead, the utility company will connect the renewable energy system to the grid.

You should check the performance of the complete system carefully, preferably before making final payments to your installers and contractors.

Once this is done, sit back and watch the energy savings roll in.

4.2   The Planning Process

The rest of this chapter provides step-by-step guidance for planning your renewal energy project. This is very important because, unless your plans are really good, you will not achieve very much.

Note this chapter deals only with the planning stage – you are not yet ready to design and build your project. During planning, you will understand the energy marketplace, assess your home's energy consumption and decide what type of renewable energy project is best suited to your needs. You will figure out what are the constraints, or limitations that will affect your choice, such as availability of sunlight or wind power and of course, how much you are willing to spend on your renewal energy project.

By the end of the chapter, you will have a much better idea of what you plan to do, so you can move on to the design/development stage of the project.

During the planning stage, the objective is to help you take some preliminary decisions about your project. This includes:

✓ Deciding what type of project you will install i.e. solar photovoltaic, solar heating or wind energy,etc.

✓ Finding out the incentives that will be available for your project i.e. FITs, Net Metering etc.

✓ Collecting data on your actual electricity consumption

✓ Deciding what percent of your home energy consumption will be met from the renewable energy project

Step 1: Choose Your Renewal Energy Project

There are several choices for the type renewal energy projects you can install in your home:

1. Solar electricity
2. Solar heating
3. Wind power
4. Water power
5. Bio-mass
6. Hybrid systems

If you live in an urban area, and you have a roof over your head, chances are that you will opt for a solar electricity project. These projects are the easiest to set-up and require no maintenance once they are operational. Also, there are no noise or air pollution issues.

In addition, the incentive programs such as FITs offering excellent rates for solar photovoltaic (PV) panels – a little better than for other renewable energy systems such as wind power. The only drawback to solar PV systems is the higher price tag, especially if you do a comparison with a solar heating systems.

However, solar heating systems are mechanically complicated. I am a mechanical engineer but I don't really favour any mechanical system that has serious maintenance issues. You have to be quite a bit of a mechanic to work with any solar heating systems.

For the average city dweller, there is little point in installing a complex mechanical system that involves piping running all over the home, heating tanks and a pump or two. If, however, you live away from the city, or own a cottage in a remote community, solar heating systems may be the right fit for you.

Again, for city dwellers, using wind power is not a good option, at least with currently available technology. Windmills do generate some noise and it is pretty unlikely that you will get permission from your city to install one in an urban area.

However, the technology is advancing rapidly and there is a new generation of windmills with horizontal blades now on the market. These devices generate less noise and have other advantages when used in urban areas. They are being used more and more in urban areas.

One example is the Best Buy building in Minneapolis where a demonstration project is currently being set-up. If this project is successful, Best Buy could set up similar projects in other stores.

So, we simply cannot rule out wind energy use in urban areas. However, the wind energy potential in your area has to be assessed carefully if you are considering its use.

Waterpower may be a viable option in some cases i.e. if you have a stream running through your property or you have a waterfront property. Technologies like biomass find limited application in homes, but there are always exceptions to any statement.

Sometimes, a hybrid system using more than one RE systemwill give you the best of two worlds. For example, you may combine a solar PV system with a windmill on your property, if you live far in a remote community. The solar panels will generate plenty of electricity during the peak summer months while the wind turbines will generate power throughout the winter.

Exercise 4-1: Selection of RE technology

Sample Project: Located in Ottawa, Ontario in a residential area

Objective: To select the appropriate renewable energy technology

Analysis:

The use of wind power is ruled out, as this is a populated area.

Other forms of renewable energy are also ruled out, as there is no biomass or bio-waste. There is no source of waterpower.

Solar heating is not a good option because the existing storage water heater runs from natural gas and is very cost effective.

There is adequate roof area for installing solar electric panels.

Also, since the house is located within Ontario, the Feed- in tariff program is applicable.

Result:

Producing solar electricity seems to be the best option.

Step 2: Know Your Incentives

Design your renewal energy project around the incentives and not the other way around. Don't install a few photovoltaic panels or a wind turbine and then look around for incentives to cover part of the costs – this is an easy way to lose money. This book is all about *saving* money through renewable energy projects and not about *spending* more money.

If you live in Ontario, you have access to one of the best incentive programs in the world: the Feed-In – Tariff (FIT) program, where the utility pays you a premium for producing renewal energy. To benefit from this program, you will have to sign a long-term contract with the local utility company, which also guarantees a steady return on investment.

Table 4-1:Ontario's Feed-in Tariff for Projects 10 KW or less			
source :OPA web-site			
Renewable technology	**Rate, cents/KW H**	**Contract term, Years**	**Escalati -on***
Solar PV	80.2	20	0%
Wind	13.5	20	20%
Waterpower	13.1	40	20%
Biomass	13.8	20	20%
Biogas	16.8	20	20%
Landfill gas	11.1	20	20%

*Escalation shows the percentage of the rate will increase annually based on consumer price index. For example, for a wind energy project, 20% of the FIT is linked to the consumer price index.

For most homeowners the items of interest are solar photovoltaic, wind energy and, possibly, waterpower.

Feed-In Tariffs for other regions in North America are summarized in Table 4-2.

Table 4-2: North America's Feed-in Tariffs			
State	**Rate, US $/KWH**	**Contract term, Years**	**Comments**
Alabama	$0.12/KWh		
California	Up to $0.16/KHh	10-25 years	

Table 4-2: **North America's Feed in Tariffs (Continued)**

State	Rate, US $/KWH	Contract term, Years	Comments
Georgia	$0.18/KHh		
Idaho	$0.02/KHh		Called production incentive
Illinois	$0.065/KHh		
Kentucky	$1000.00 + $0.12/KWh		
Michigan	$0.65/KWh	12 years	
Minnesota	Up to $1.00/KWh		
Missouri	$1000.00 + $0.12/KWh		
New Jersey	Up to $0.69/KWh		
New Mexico	$0.13/KHh	12 years	
North Carolina	$0.18/KHh	20 years	
Texas	Up to 10% over retail rate		
Vermont	0.30	20	
Virginia	$1000.00 + $0.12/KWh		

As this table shows, only a handful of North American states have Feed-in Tariff programs. Most of the others have Net Metering programs.

There may also be other incentives tied in to the

capital cost of the project. Also, check if you get any other rebates or tax credits for renewable energy projects. Many homes in Canada are eligible for a Home Improvement Tax Credit.

Find out what these programs are and how you can benefit from them. It is important to do this research as part of the planning process for your project.

Exercise 4-2:Applicable Feed-in Tariff

Sample Project: Located in Ottawa, Ontario in a residential area
Objective: To select the appropriate renewable energy technology
Analysis
Since the project is in Ontario and it is likely to be less than 5KW, the applicable microFIT tariff is $0.80/KWh.
Result
Applicable Feed-in Tariff: $0.80/KWH

Step 3: Check for Local Content

Some jurisdictions have a requirement for local content tied in to their renewable energy incentive programs. If you do not meet this condition, you will not be eligible for the incentive program.

For example, Ontario's latest FIT program, introduced in 2009, requires at least 40% local content. Earlier incentive programs in Ontario did not have this requirement. Quite a few people were taken aback, because some had already set-up projects using suppliers from outside the province.

Suddenly, they found they would not qualify for the latest incentives. So it is good to do your homework before you start the project.

In general, it is not very difficult to meet the local content requirement, because the work done by energy consultants and by installers also counts towards local content. So even if you buy some components from outside the province, you can still meet the minimum local content requirements.

Also, in Ontario, the current requirement for local content is 40% Ontario for projects completed before end of 2010; thereafter, the rate will increase to 60%. Hence it makes sense to start your project now and complete it before the end of 2010.

Other jurisdictions may have different ideas. Make sure that you study the requirements for local content carefully before embarking on your project.

As the example below shows, meeting the local content requirement is fairly easy to meet. However, if you built a project *before* this requirement came into effect, you could be in trouble.

Exercise 4-3: Local content requirements

Sample Project: Located in Ottawa, Ontario in a residential area
Objective: To determine local content
Type of project: Rooftop Solar PV panels
Analysis:
Since the project is in Ontario, a minimum of 40% local content is required.

This will be met as follows:

Photovoltaic panels: Source not known, at this stage

Inverter:	Ontario source,	9%
Wiring etc.	Ontario source,	10%
Labour	Ontario source,	27%
Total		**46%**

Results:

At the planning stage, it appears the project will meet local content requirement.

Step 4: Estimate Cost of Energy

The objective of this step is to get some ballpark estimates of renewable energy costs in dollars per watt. This is a tricky step, but even at this early stage of the game, you need some idea of how much renewable energy will cost. At this stage, you cannot get a very accurate estimate; that will come a little later. The initial estimate will be refined further as the design proceeds.

First, you need a ballpark estimate of the cost of renewable energy in $/KWH. Costs keep changing all the time but at the time of writing (2009), the cost for a residential solar panel varies is US $4.38 /Watt, according to the web-site solar buzz, which tracks the module processes every month.

http://www.solarbuzz.com/Moduleprices.htm

The same site lists Inverter prices at about $0.72 /watt. Another site, Ecobusiness, tracks solar module prices by manufacturer.

http://www.ecobusinesslinks.com/solar_panels.htm

According to this site, the retail price for solar panels is in the $2 to $4.65 range.

During the planning stage, we need only ballpark estimates for the cost of the project.

Taking the highest prices from these sites, the ballpark cost is estimated as:

Solar modules	$4.65/watt
Inverter	$0.72/watt
Total	$5.37/watt

The solar module and the inverter represent the two major pieces of equipment in a solar photovoltaic system. There are additional costs for disconnects, wiring, junction boxes, fuses and other required safety devices. There are also installation costs and payments for inspections, permits etc. Also, the costs will have to be converted into Canadian dollars for our readers north of the border.

Hence, the actual cost for a complete system may be almost double. This gives a ballpark figure of CAN $10/watt.

Is this a reasonable estimate? To find out, we checked prices with an Ontario installer of solar photovoltaic panels. The price ranged from $9-11/watt, depending upon the size of the installation. Hence, it appears that $10/watt is a reasonable estimate for a solar photovoltaic system in Ontario.

These costs, do, however, change with time. So it is best to do good research before starting your project. Luckily, there are plenty of web resources for getting more information; the web sites listed in Chapter 11 are a good starting point.

The cost of wind generators varies from US$1.5 to $2.5/watt, according to *The Homeowner's Guide to Renewable Energy* 2006. However, this figure covers only the cost of the wind turbines. There are additional costs for the windmill tower, foundation, the inverter and other electrical components. The total installed costs vary considerably from manufacturer to manufacturer. According to the 2005 data given in the book, the price is $8 to $15 per watt. Today's market conditions are likely to be different.

Hence a good ballpark figure for wind energy cost estimation is US$15/watt. However, this is based on data that is already four years' old.

We have no cost estimates for other types of renewable energy such as solar heating systems or micro-hydroelectric projects as the systems vary too much with site conditions. However, *The Homeowner's Guide to Renewable Energy* does provide some useful information.

Step 5: Check Renewable Energy Potential

The objective of this step is to estimate the maximum amount of renewable energy your home can generate, given its size limitations. In the case of solar PV panels, check how much useful roof area you have, if you plan a rooftop installation. The useful roof area will put an upper limit on the maximum capacity that you can install.

Solar PV panels work best on a south-facing roof or wall where they get the maximum sunshine. Even a small amount of shade can reduce energy production substantially. Even if one or two cells are shaded in a panel, that panel may stop producing electricity. This is because individual cells are connected in series inside the panel; hence if any one panel breaks down the entire panel can stop producing electricity.

Some panel manufacturers do try to solve this problem by using protective diodes. These devices are connected in parallel to the cell wiring, but in reverse. If any cell breaks down due to shading, its output is bypassed by the protective diode; effectively, this allows the rest of the panel to keep on producing electricity. However, the shaded cell will not produce any output.

So check how much of the roof is shaded and how much is actually available for solar energy generation.

Next calculate how much solar power you can generate from the given collection area. Each manufacturer has different specifications so the output in KW per unit area will vary. We studied the specifications of a number of manufacturers and came up with the following estimate:

Rule Of Thumb:
A solar panel can generate approximately 11 watts/sq.ft.

Use this rule only for estimation purposes. If you want better accuracy, look at the actual manufacturer's specifications before starting your project.

Hence if your usable roof area is 500 sq.ft, the maximum solar energy you can produce is about 5 KW. Just note that this is only a possible maximum; the actual generation may be much less, due to other installation constraints.

Another factor to consider is how you will install the solar panels, as this will also affect solar power availability. The most important variable is the tilt angle i.e. the angle between the panel and the horizontal plane.

In many cases, the panels will be installed directly on the roof. Hence, the angle of tilt of the panels will equal the slope of the roof. As we explain in the next chapter, the optimal tilt angle equals the latitude of the project site. Hence, if the project is in Ottawa, Canada you need a tilt angle of 46 degrees for best results. If the actual tilt angle is off by about 15 degrees, allow for a 20% reduction in panel efficiency.

Another important variable is the panel orientation. The array will work at maximum efficiency if it faces exactly due south; any deviation from this will reduce the output. If the orientation is 5 degrees from due south, expect a reduction of about 5%.
Note that the panels will operate at the rated efficiency only during peak daylight hours. Hence you will need to calculate the availability of sunlight at your location; we will explain this process during step 7.

It is helpful to get a photograph of your home and use this to calculate the roof area. Use easily measured objects such as window frames to scale the photograph. With today's technology, you may not even have to take a picture of your house as it might be available from a number of web resources. Try google maps; if you enter your address, you will get a map of your area; just click on your home and go to Street view to get a series of pictures of your home. This works only in areas where google has collected the data.

Some municipalities also have house pictures on records that can be accessed using the Internet. For example, if you live in Ottawa, try the following website:

http://apps104.ottawa.ca/emap/

Exercise 4-4:Maximum project capacity

Sample Project: Located in Ottawa, Ontario
Objective: To estimate maximum possible capacity of project
Description: The property is a three-bedroom house with south facing bedroom windows.
There are two levels of roof: above the bedroom level and just below the bedroom level.
The home was built about 20 years back; drawings for the home are not readily available.
However, simple measurements using a tape measure from the bedroom window indicate that the lower level south-facing roof measures about 12 ft by 24 ft.
The upper roof is at least this big, if not larger.
Visual inspection indicates the slope is 30 degrees

for lower roof and 40 degrees for upper roof.
Analysis
From these dimensions, it is estimated that the south facing roof area is at least 576 sq.ft.
Hence the maximum capacity of solar panels =11 x 576 watts = 11x 576/1000 KW =6.3 KW
This capacity is reduced due to shading and due to non-optimal tilt angle. Hence the actual capacity may be 20-30% less i.e. about 4.4 KW.
Results
Maximum capacity : 4.4 KW

Step 6:Estimate Electrical Load

The previous chapter explained how your utility bill is set-up. The utility bill should provide you with the following information to complete step 6:

1. Your average yearly, monthly and daily consumption of electricity.
2. Your average power consumption per hour, in KW. Obtain this figure by dividing the daily consumption by 24 i.e. the number of hours in a day.

Exercise 4-5: Electricity consumption data

Sample Project: Located in Ottawa, Ontario
Objective: Report electricity consumption data
Results
From Chapter 3 Sample Project data
Average Monthly Consumption = 414 KWh
Average Annual Consumption = 4971 KWh
Average Consumption/day =13.6KWH/day
Average Consumption/hour = 0.57 KW

Average Electrical load   = 0.57 KW

Step 7: Size Your System

Sizing your renewal energy system may require several rounds of calculations, as a number of factors have to be balanced against each other. The system capacity has to be balanced against your budget constraints i.e. how much you are willing to spend on the project. If the project cost turns out to be high, you may want to go for a smaller system, or, even, do the project in two or three stages.

There may be other constraints, also, such as noise issues that could limit the size of the project. You may even decide to spend more than the initial budget because larger projects are definitely more efficient and yield better returns. All in all, it is a fine balancing act, which only you, the owner can perform correctly.

The discussion below centres around solar photovoltaic panels, but the same logical process can be applied to other forms of renewable energy such as wind or waterpower.

The starting point is to figure out how much solar energy your location receives. This data is available from various government web sites but each site uses its own nomenclature. Hence it is important to understand some of the terminology used.

Some sites give the information is often given in the form of **peak sun hours**. In simple terms, the peak sun hours tell us how many usable hours of sunlight the site will get; this information can be given for each month or as an average for the entire year.

Sometimes, the data is given using the term **insolation**. The solar energy striking the earth's surface at a given time and place is called **insolation.** It is expressed in units of energy per unit area. In the metric system this is watts/sq. m or kilowatts/sq.m. Other units that are in use include BTUs/sq.ft, joules/sq.ft, Langleys or peak sun hour. In this book, we will use W/sq.m. or KW/Sq.m.

> **Insolation can readily be converted into peak sun hours using the following equation:**
> **1KW/Sq.M = 1000 watts/sq.M = 1 peak sun hour.**

In other words, **peak sun hours** are the number of hours per day when the solar insolation equals 1KW/sq.m.

Solar energy data for the US is available from the web site:

http://www.solar4power.com/solar-power-insolation.html

This site lists insolation data for most major US cities, in the form of high, low and average insolation values. The units for this data are sun-hours/day i.e. the peak sun hours.

Solar energy data for Canada is available from the web site:

https://glfc.cfsnet.nfis.org/mapserver/pv/municip.ph
p?n=1408&lang=e

The Canadian web site uses a very different format from the US web sites and provides more detailed information. There are also more steps involved in getting the data that you need.

First, you need to enter your location; this you will take you to a set of tables for that site. Just look at the last table in the set; it will show the mean daily global insolation in KWh/sq.metres for a number of different solar panel orientations. For the planning stage, look only at the data for south facing arrays with tilt angle equal to the altitude. These values are given in KWh/sq.metres which is essentially the same number as the peak sun hours shown in the US web site.

For example, look up the data for Ottawa, Ontario. The last table lists a mean insolation of 4.4 KWh/sq.m for a south-facing array with a tilt angle equal to the altitude. This simply means that, if you install a solar PV panel with a capacity of 1KW, it will, on an average, generate 4.4 KWh per day in Ottawa.

Now, we have all the information required for preliminary sizing of the solar array. Use the following equation to calculate the capacity of the solar photovoltaic panel that meets 100% of the residential electrical load:

CS = EC/INS   (1)
       Where,
       CS= Capacity of solar photovoltaic panel, in

KW
EC = Capacity of existing residential electrical system in KWh/day
INS = Insolation, in kWh/sq.metres or, in Peak Sun Hours.

As an example, let us apply this equation to a home in Ottawa with an residential electrical system that produces 10 KWh/day.

For Ottawa, the insolation is 4.4 kWh/sq.metres.

From Equation 1,

CS = 10 / 4.4 = 2.3 KW.

Thus, we need to install a 2.3 KW solar photovoltaic panel to meet 100% of the home's electricity needs.

Once you know the capacity of the system, you will probably need an estimate of how much it will cost. Use the rule of thumb given in Step 4 ; the cost is approximately $10/watt. For the present exercise,
Cost = CS*1000*10 =23000

Hence the estimated cost is approximately $23,000.00

You may find this cost is way over your budget. Do not despair; see if you are comfortable with a smaller system to bring the costs down to a manageable level. So you might have to play with the size of the solar array a little bit, until you get a size that you can live with.

In you want to put in a smaller system, use the following equation to estimate the capacity:

$$CS = F * EC/INS \qquad (2)$$

Where

F= Fraction of total load that will be met from the solar PV panel.

For example, if you want to meet only 50% of the load from solar PV panels, F=0.5

Hence, from equation (2),

$$CS = .5*10/4.4 = 1.15 \text{ KW}$$

The cost for this system is given by:

$$Cost = CS*1000*10 = 11500$$

Hence the cost is $11,500.00

If you want to bring the costs down still further, consider a smaller system, with F =0.25. Now,

$$CS = .25*10/4.4 = 0.53 \text{ KW}$$

For this system, the approximate cost is estimated at $5,300.

The actual cost may be a little higher because smaller systems do cost a little more per KW.

With this information, you can now take a better decision on the size of your renewal energy project. If the costs are still too high, you might even decide to do the project in two or three stages.

However, dividing the project into several stages may push up the total cost because you no longer get the economy of scale.

Exercise 4-6:Sizing the RE system

Sample Project: Located in Ottawa, Ontario

Objective: Size the RE system

Analysis
Electricity Consumption/day = 13.6 KWH/day, from previous analysis
For Ottawa, Average Insolation = 4.4 KWH/sq.m
If 100% of the load is met from solar electricity,
Required capacity = 13.6/4.4 = 3.1 KW
Cost = 3.1 * 10*1000 = $31,000.00
If 50% of load is met from solar electricity,
Required Capacity = 13.6/4.4*0.5 = 1.55 KW
Cost = 1.55*10*1000 = $15,500.00
If 25% of load is met from solar electricity,
Required capacity = 13.6*.25/4.4 = 0.77 KW
Cost = 0.77*10*1000 = $7,700.00

Results
Based on this analysis, the owner decides to take the middle path and install
a capacity of 1.55 KW.

Step 8: Check Panel Weight

During this step, you should examine any other factors that might limit the size of your project. Consider the weight of the solar panels – will the roof be able to sustain this weight on a long-term basis?

To help you find out, do a little analysis of panel weights and capacities. For this, you will to look at the manufacturer's specifications. This is difficult at this stage, because you don't know which manufacturer will offer you the best deal. So, we did a little research of our own and came up with a rule of thumb for panel weight:

> **Rule Of Thumb:**
> **A solar panel will generate approximately 10 watts/kg**

Hence, the weight of the solar panels will be:

$W = CS* 100$
Where
W = weight in kg; and CS = capacity of solar panel in KW.
For example, if the panels have a capacity of 1 KW,
$W = 1*100 = 100$ kg

Now you need to decide if the roof can support this weight. At first glance, it appears that weight will not be a problem because a 100 kg person can easily walk on the roof. Also, the weight is distributed over the entire sun-facing rooftop.

However, it might be worthwhile to re-visit the weight issue during the design development stage.

Exercise 4-7:Check Panel Weight

Sample Project: Located in Ottawa, Ontario
Objective: To check panel weight
Analysis
Capacity = 1.55 KW, from previous analysis

Weight = 1.55*100 = 155 kg
This weight will be distributed over a roof two roof tops.
Hence, the weight on individual roof would be about 78 kg.
Results
This appears to be a reasonable weight for the roof to carry, subject to further verification during the design development stage.

Step 9: Calculate Returns

The return on investment can be calculated in a number of ways. You could do a rate of return analysis, or a simple payback analysis that calculates the number of years it takes to pay back the investment.

There are more complex types of cost/benefit analyses that can be done; however, unless you are an economist, you don't really need to go there for a small home renewal energy project.

The rate of return is simply the annual revenue from the investment divided by the project cost, expressed as a percentage. For example, if a project costs $10,000 and generates revenue of $1000 per year, the rate of return is 1000/10000* 100 = 10% per year. For the purpose of this book, we do not consider the cost of the land or building; it is assumed you already own it. Also, we do not consider the cost of borrowing money as we want to keep the analysis as simple as possible and the idea is only to *compare* various alternatives.

The simple payback is the number of years it takes

to pay for the investment, again without considering the cost of the money. For example, if a project costs $10,000 and generates a revenue of $1000 per year, the simple payback time is 10,000/1000 = 10 years.

In this book, we'll only give you the simplest formulae that you can readily apply for your simple renewable energy project.

$$ROR = R/C * 100 \qquad\qquad (3)$$
And
$$SP = C/R \qquad\qquad (4)$$

Where ROI	=	Rate of return, %
R	=	Annual revenue
C	=	Project Cost in dollars
SP	=	Simple payback

For home renewable energy projects the rate of return is high, because the owner does not have to pay for the space that he already owns. This for a roof-top solar PV project, there is no extra cost for the roof. As a result the rate of return is much higher than for a commercial project where the developed has to buy the land to set up the project. For the same reason, the payback period is very short.

However, there may be tax implications that would have to be analyzed separately. This will depend upon how the project is set up and the individual's tax bracket. For example, it might be beneficial, in some cases, to set up a separate business entity for the project where various business expenses and depreciation could be deducted.

Exercise 4-8:Return on Investment

Sample Project: Located in Ottawa, Ontario
Objective: To calculate return on investment
Analysis
Capacity of Project = 1.55 KW
Estimated Cost of Project = $ 15,500
Average Insolation = 4.4 hours/day
Number of days/year = 365 (rounded off)
Hence, Annual Electricity Output = 1.55*4.4*365 =2489 KWh/year
Applicable Feed In Tariff =$ 0.80 /KWH
Hence, annual revenue = 0.80*2489 = $1991 per year
Results
Rate of return =1991/15500*100 =13 %
Simple payback = 15500/1991 =7.8 years

Step 10: Check Impact on Home Value

It seems intuitive to believe that home resale values go up when solar PV panels are installed. Who would *not* want to buy home where there are no utility bills to pay?

However, do talk to a realtor, if you can, to see what is the impact of the renewable energy project in your home. Chances are, the home value will go up once you install a renewable energy system.

You may also want to check if the house tax will go up, if you install a renewable energy system. For this, you should contact the municipal authority responsible for house tax assessments.

Step 11: Check Regulations

Any changes to the home may require changes to building permit. Clearances may be required from environmental agencies if you install, for example, a wind generator. In built-up areas, city by-laws may prohibit use of wind energy. We will go into this subject in more detail in Chapter 5 where we talk about the approval process.

At this stage, the intent is only to find out if there is any regulation that will prevent you from doing this project. For example, if you plan to install a wind mill, there may be by-laws that ban this application in your neighbourhood. There may also by-laws against noise pollution in your locality.

Step 12: Document Your Plan

We suggest using a spreadsheet to document the key elements of your plan. One suggested format is given in Table 4-3 but you can always choose another format that you find more convenient. The important thing is to have a document that evolves as you proceed towards completing the project.

Table 4-3: Project Plan		
Step	Name	Activity
1	Choose Your Project	Evaluate various RE technologies
2	Know Your Incentives	Find applicable incentive
3	Check For Local content	Check if requirements are met
4	Estimate Renewable Energy (RE) Cost	Get ballpark figures for RE cost

5	Check Home's Renewable Energy Potential	Check available area for RE system
6	Estimate Home's Electrical Load	Compute residential load in KW
7	Size The Renewable energy System	Select appropriate size of system
8	Check panel weight	Check if weight is excessive
9	Calculate return in investment	Calculate rate of Return, Simple Payback
10	Check Impact On Home value	Check if home value goes up with RE
11	Check laws & regulations	Check if any laws/regulations will prohibit RE project

Chapter 5: Design Your Photovoltaic System

Contents

5.1	The Design Phase
5.2	Photovoltaic System Fundamentals
5.3	Solar Energy Fundamentals
5.4	Locating Your Photovoltaic Panels
5.5	Sizing Your Panels
5.6	Panel Mounting Options
5.7	Inverter selection
5.8	Disconnect Selection
5.9	Wiring Selection
5.10	Other Accessories
5.11	Prepare Schematics
5.12	Prepare Bill of Materials
5.13	Verify All Details
5.14	Solar Photovoltaic Kits

5.1 The Design Phase

After completing your planning, you can begin the design phase of your solar photovoltaic system. By this time, you have a good idea of what you want to do, how much it will cost and what the benefits will be.

You know the approximate capacity of your project, based on the limitations of the size of your home and your budget. So far, you haven't looked at any of the components that make up the solar photovoltaic system at any level of detail.

Next you enter the design phase; this is where the rubber hits the road and your project really takes off. Now you get into all the details that are required to make the project work. For this phase, you will need to know a bit more about how photovoltaic systems work and how the various components are interconnected.

By the time you complete this phase, you will have ironed out all the details and your project will be ready to go, subject, of course, to approval by the authorities. You will have a much better idea of project cost.

Once this is done, there remains one final detail: buying all the components and installing them. This final implementation phase will be a piece of cake if you have done the previous stages correctly. By following a planned process for setting up your project you will ensure that everything goes through without a hitch. You will save tons of money, because you will pay your professional consultants, installers and electricians only for specific tasks that you cannot do on your own.

Also, by doing your own planning and design, you will be in the driver's seat, not your consultant or advisor.

You might notice the number of exercises dwindle as you work your way through the Chapter 5. There is a very good reason for that: as the design develops, it gets more vendor-specific. We don't want to give examples where vendor names are mentioned, as this might be construed as an endorsement of a particular product or manufacturer.

Also, if we show you a fully designed system as an example, you might be tempted to use exactly that design for your project. That can lead to all kinds of problems because no one design can fit all applications.

5.2 Photovoltaic System Fundamentals

This section provides a little background on how photovoltaic systems work. You don't need to be an expert but a little understanding of these systems is always beneficial.

Photovoltaic (PV) systems convert solar energy directly into electricity. They are clean and reliable systems that emit no pollutants. They have been used successfully in a wide variety of applications and you will probably find a photovoltaic device in your light-powered calculator that never requires a battery.

The basic building block unit of all these systems is a photovoltaic cell - a thin disc of semi-conducting material that generates electricity when exposed to light.

Silicon is the most commonly used semiconductor material for PV applications. It is one of the most abundant elements on the earth's surface; ordinary sand contains plenty of silicon, trapped as an oxide. Silica is another common mineral containing silicon. However, the element requires extensive processing before it can use in a photovoltaic application and this is what makes these silicon chips so expensive.

For use in photovoltaic systems, raw silicon has to be refined to an ultra-pure state, when it becomes a semi-conductor, a type of material that is half way between an insulator and a conductor of electricity. Just as a refresher for those unfamiliar with Electronics 101, insulators do not conduct electricity at all, while conductors do so freely.

Semiconductors do conduct electricity but the resistance is very high. Also, they conduct more electricity in one direction than in the other, forming what is known as the p-n junction. Semiconductors are the basic building blocks of electronic components such as transistors. Some semiconductors are light sensitive and convert light to electricity; these are the types used in solar photovoltaic panels.

After silicon has been purified it is grown into crystals and "doped" with a material such as phosphorous, to give it semiconductor properties. Doping is essentially a very carefully controlled process of deliberately adding an impurity to the semi-conductor material.

There are essentially three types of photovoltaic cells:

- ❖ Polycrystalline,
- ❖ Single crystals and
- ❖ Amorphous.

The polycrystalline form has the highest solar conversion efficiency; it consists of a number of crystals grown together using a special process. Single crystal types have slightly lower efficiency while the amorphous type has about half the efficiency of the other types. Home solar panels generally use single crystalline or amorphous type silicon cells, as these are the most economical. Conversion efficiency ranges from 14% to 20%. The photovoltaic material is generally laminated on one side of the cell with a clear substrate on the other side.

A single cell does not produce appreciable power, so a number of photovoltaic cells are joined together. This forms a photovoltaic panel. Typically, a photovoltaic panel contains about a hundred cells. Very often, the terms "panel" and "module" are used interchangeably.

When one or more panels are wired together, it is called an array. The array produces usable electricity, generally in the 10-40 Volts DC range. The photovoltaic modules are connected together using low voltage wiring.

Performance of solar panels is generally expressed as a P-V curve, which shows the relationship between voltage and current. The voltage is highest at zero current i.e. when there is no load or, nothing is connected on the output side. As current rises and the system draws more power, the voltage drops. The power output at any point on the P-V curve is calculated by multiplying the voltage by the current.

Photovoltaic panels cells are tested in the factory only at certain standard conditions that consist of an insolation rate of 1000 watts/square metre, at an ambient temperature of 25 degrees C, amongst other test parameters.

In an actual installation, the efficiency never equals the manufacturers' values, because field conditions are always very different. Hence it is important to estimate how the well the panel will perform in real life by considering all the factors that affect its performance. They include:

1. The strength of the sunlight at that location.
2. Tilt angle
3. Shading effects

These factors were discussed in the previous sections. In addition, module temperature also has an effect on panel performance.

As module temperature rises, the efficiency drops.

At temperatures of about 50 degree C, the performance can degrade by as much as 20%. In cold countries like Canada, the panel temperature rarely exceeds 30 deg.C and the photovoltaic panels will perform quite well.

The temperature effect also leads to a strange anomaly, as some researchers have reported. Solar PV systems may work at a higher efficiency in Canada than in the hottest parts of the USA. One researcher compared PV performance at a site in Arizona with the performance in Toronto, Canada. The panels run at a 20 deg.C lower temperature in Toronto as compared to Arizona, where the panel temperature could go up to 50 deg.C during summer. As a result, the Toronto installation was found to be 20% more efficient.

Another major component of a PV system is the combiner box. Modules are commonly connected into an electrical string to produce the desired voltage and amperage. The resulting wires from each string are routed to the combiner box. In this box all the strings are combined into one electrical output which is then fed to the inverter.

Solar PV panels produce only direct current (DC). This is the type of current produced in cells and batteries, as opposed to the Alternating Current (AC) that flows through power grids. Hence the DC output from the photovoltaic panel needs to be converted to AC; this is accomplished using a device called an inverter.

The inverter, essentially, takes a low voltage DC signal and converts it to a higher voltage AC signal.

Thus it forms the interface between your solar photovoltaic device and the power grid. The inverter also performs other functions, such as matching the frequency of the AC signal produced to the power grid frequency. Most inverters are solid-state devices i.e. they have no moving parts. As a result a correctly sized inverter is a very reliable piece of equipment.

Inverters are of various types. Some systems use "stand-alone" inverters that essentially, supply power to various home appliances and are not connected to the grid. Others connect to the grid; these are often called "grid-tie" inverters. They are generally required to supply a higher quality of power that matches the quality obtained from the grid. In addition, the "grid-tie" inverters match the frequency and phase of the power from the grid. Hence, they deliver power synchronized with the grid.

Don't worry if this information is too technical; all you really need to know, really, is to specify "grid-tie" inverters for solar photovoltaic systems, if they will be connected to the grid.

Another element in the solar PV system is the "smart" meter; this is required when using Feed-in Tariff. This device measures power consumption in reverse i.e. when it is being fed into the power grid. The utility company provides the smart meter. Once your solar PV system is approved for installation, the smart meter will be provided at no extra cost.

In addition, there is wiring for the solar PV system and this again, is not your common, garden variety of wiring. There are in fact, two circuits involved: low voltage wiring, up to the input to the inverter and high voltage wiring between the inverter and the grid.

All wiring on the roof and outside the house must be weatherproof and must meet the required standards for outdoor wiring. This type of wiring is generally placed inside a conduit. Wiring inside the house need not be weatherproof but it must meet a host of safety standards, as we will describe later

The inverter and the smart meter should be installed as close to the existing meter connection as possible. In many cases, it is possible to install them outside the house, at the point where the grid connects to the home. If this is done, all the wiring for the solar PV system will be outside the house.

If you look at any other book on photovoltaics or on renewable energy you will probably see plenty of information on power storage devices such as batteries. Just ignore it; the approach we advocate does not require batteries at all, since the system is tied to the power grid. The grid itself serves as a huge energy storage device, providing the power whenever needed. Our approach – why re-invent the wheel?

Batteries are useful only if you do not want to connect to the grid. We also do not advocate off the grid living because it is very expensive and you need to maintain a complete battery back-up system. Off the grid living is fit only for the adventurous who also happen to be good handymen. With the development of Feed-In-Tariffs, off the grid living is unnecessary because there is more money to be made by connecting your renewable energy system to the grid.

However, there are some cases where it might be cheaper to generate your own renewable power than it is to connect to the grid. If you decide to build a home more than, say, five kilometres from a power line, the utility may charge too much money for bringing the power to your house.

In such cases, you may want to invest in a major renewable energy project to meet 100% of your energy needs. But be prepared – you will have to invest in a battery system also and you should be prepared for a heavy dose of maintenance activities throughout the life of your project.

If you use batteries you will also need a controller, to maintain the proper charging conditions for the battery. This device automatically reduces the current as the battery approaches a fully charged state. The commonest type of battery used in solar photovoltaic systems is the lead-acid battery, much like the ones used in automobiles.

Yet another essential component of the photovoltaic system is the disconnect switch, provided between the inverter and the power grid meter. The disconnect switch is required to isolate the solar photovoltaic system from the power grid whenever required. Hence, if the solar PV system fails for any reason, it can be quickly disconnected.

The utility company generally requires that the disconnect switch for the solar PV system should be located in a place readily accessible to utility personnel. Using a disconnect switch is a legal requirement for connecting to the utility grid.

In addition to these major components, the solar photovoltaic system requires a number of minor pieces of equipment. These include over-current protection devices, lightning protectors and various other safety devices. The use of most of these devices is mandated by code.

The components of a typical solar PV system connected to the power grid are shown below. This type of system is generally referred to as a grid inter-tie system or, a grid-interactive system.

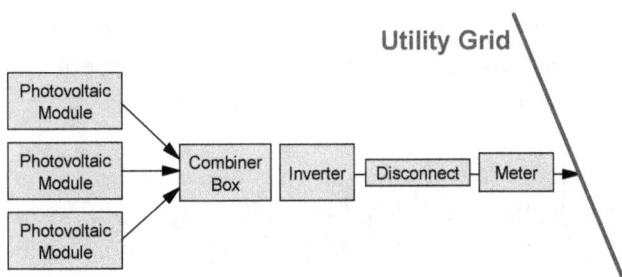

Figure 5-1: Grid Intertie System

5.3   Solar Energy Fundamentals

Solar photovoltaic devices capture the sun's energy which is abundantly available on the earth's surface; of course only a minuscule fraction of this energy stream is normally captured. Typically, a solar PV panel operates at 15-20% efficiency; more efficient devices with a conversion efficiency of up to 40% have been developed but they normally cost far too much to be viable. This means that, at best, you can recover 40% of the solar energy that falls on a PV panel.

As we discussed briefly in the previous chapter, the solar energy striking the earth's surface at a given time and place is called **insolation.** Generally, its value is expressed in units of energy per unit area. In the metric system this is watts/sq. m or kilowatts/sq.m. Other units that are in use include BTUs/sq.ft, joules/sq.ft, Langleys or peak sun hour. In this book, we will use W/sq.m. Also note the following equivalence:

1KW/Sq.M = 1000 watts/sq.M = 1 **peak sun hour**.

In other words, **peak sun hours** are the number of hours per day when the solar insolation equals 1000W/sq.m.

On a clear day, the total insolation striking the earth's surface is 1 KW/Sq. metre or, 1 peak sun hour. Insolation is affected by atmospheric conditions such as the presence of dust, water vapour and carbon dioxide.

If you live in the Northern hemisphere, the sun will be seen mostly in the southern sky. It will rise towards the east, follow a southerly arc, and set towards the west; the exact path will vary with the time of the year.

At the equator, the sun is directly overhead at noon as you might recall from geography 101. In the Southern hemisphere, the conditions are reversed and the sun follows a northerly arc.

Why do we need to know all this stuff? It is important because it affects how well a solar photovoltaic panel performs under different conditions.

It is also important to know the difference between true south and magnetic south. If you look at a map, the direction marked as south is the true south. However, if you use a compass, the direction you see is actually the magnetic south. This is not the same as the true south shown on the map. The difference between the two values is called the magnetic declination and it is measured in degrees. It varies from place to place and a declination map gives the variation.

So why are terms like true south, magnetic south and declination important in the design of solar photovoltaic systems? They are important because you would normally use a magnetic compass when surveying your site to find out the path of the sun. Declination is important for correcting the compass reading to find true south.

For optimum performance, solar PV arrays must face as close to due south as possible. If the array is off by 15 degrees from due south it will, typically, lose 10% efficiency i.e. it will collect only 90% of the available solar energy.

The next important factor to consider is the solar array's **tilt angle** i.e. the angle between the horizontal and the plane of the photovoltaic array. If the tilt angle is horizontal, or vertical, the sun's rays will fall at an oblique angle and the panel's efficiency will be reduced. Efficiency is highest when the rays of the sun strike perpendicular to the plane of the array. Hence there is an optimum tilt angle, between the two extremes, when the panel operates at maximum efficiency.

A good year-round setting for the tilt angle is to keep it the same as the latitude. For example, Ottawa, Canada has latitude of 46 degrees. Hence the tilt angle should be 46 degrees on a year-round basis.

There is, however, also a seasonal effect since the path of the sun varies with the time of the year. Hence, a higher tilt angle is required in summer than in winter. These variations are summarized in the table below:

Table 5-1: Recommended Tilt Angles	
Season	**Tilt Angle**
Year Round	Equal to latitude
Summer	Equal to latitude minus 15 degrees
Winter	Equal to latitude plus 15 degrees

As a rule of thumb, if the tilt angle is within 15 degrees of the optimum angle, the efficiency loss should be less than 5%.

However, it may not always be feasible to adjust the tilt angle according to the season. If a panel is installed on the roof, the tilt angle cannot readily be adjusted and the system will operate at a little lower efficiency because the tilt angle is fixed throughout the year.

If the tilt angle deviates more than 15 degrees from the values shown in Table 1, expect an efficiency loss of upto 15%.

There are sophisticated **tracking systems** available for use in solar arrays. You can get a single axis or a double axis tracking system. The double axis system will track the sun's movements very precisely and ensure you get the highest possible efficiency from the solar array at all times. However, these tracking systems are expensive and they also take up space. They are useful when they form a part of a ground-mounted array; they are harder to use in a roof where the weight of the system could also pose a problem.

Finally, there is the concept of a **solar window.** This is definitely not your bedroom window –it is a specialized term used in studying the operation of solar PC panels. The solar window is the time frame for optimum collection of solar energy – your window of opportunity. In most cases, it is the time between 9 a.m. and 3:00 p.m. when you get the maximum sunlight during a 24-hour cycle.

5.4 Locating Solar Panels

During this phase, you survey the site to determine the best location and orientation for your solar array. You have already estimated the capacity of the solar PV system during the planning stage. Considering the site conditions in real detail will now further refine the estimates. The starting point for this analysis is the insolation data for your home.

We referred to insolation data very briefly in the previous chapter. Now, we get into more details.

Insolation data is available for most of the major cities in North America; weather offices and various government agencies have meticulously compiled it. All you have to do is look it up; just see the reference web sites in Chapter 9. Here is an example of the insolation data for Ottawa, Ontario:

Table 5-2: Insolation data in KWh/sq. metres

	South-facing vertical, tilt=90°	South-facing, tilt=latitude	South-facing, tilt=latitude+15°	South-facing, tilt=latitude-15°	Two-axis sun-tracking
Jan	3.6	3.4	3.6	3.0	4.2
Feb.	4.5	4.7	4.9	4.2	5.8
Mar	4.4	5.4	5.3	5.2	6.9
Apr.	3.3	5.1	4.7	5.3	7.2
May	2.8	5.1	4.5	5.5	7.8
Jun.	2.6	5.2	4.5	5.7	8.3
Jul.	2.7	5.4	4.6	5.9	8.5
Aug.	3.0	5.1	4.6	5.4	7.5
Sept.	3.1	4.4	4.2	4.4	5.9
Oct.	3.1	3.6	3.6	3.4	4.5
Nov.	2.5	2.5	2.7	2.3	3.0
Dec.	2.8	2.7	2.9	2.3	3.2
Annu-al	3.2	4.4	4.2	4.4	6.1

Source:https://glfc.cfsnet.nfis.org/mapserver/pv/municip.php?n=1408&lang=e

This table requires a few words of explanation as the data refers to six different configurations of a solar array:

1. South facing, tilt angle = 90 degrees. This is useful when you want to install the PV panel on an exterior wall.
2. South facing, tilt = latitude. This is the optimum configuration for year-round operation of the panel. This configuration is useful for solar roof top units.
3. South facing, tilt = latitude + 15 degrees. This is a good configuration for summer months, if you have a means for changing the tilt angle. This is applicable to roof top solar PV panels.
4. South facing, tilt= latitude − 15 degrees. This is a good configuration for winter months, if you have a means for changing the tilt angle. This is also applicable to roof top solar PV panels.
5. Two-axis, sun tracking. This is useful, if you have a sun-tracking device. This is generally not feasible for roof-mounted unit. You could, however, consider this option for a backyard unit, to extract the best possible performance from your solar PC array.

From this data, you can see that an array with tilt angle equal to the latitude will give best all year round performance. Also, for Ottawa, the worst performance will be during the months of November and December.

The next important thing to consider is the effect of shading. This has a major impact on the performance of the solar array. By shading, we mean the shadows cast by objects around the site on the solar panel. If any object blocks the sunlight even partially, it can have a disastrous effect on the performance of the PV panel.

The individual cells that make up the panel are generally connected in series. This means that if just one cell breaks down, or is shaded, then the output of the entire panel can be affected.

Some manufacturers try to minimize this problem by using protective diodes; these devices provide a short-circuit path for a cell that breaks down or is shaded. With this device, you can bypass a cell that has stopped functioning, so that there is no impact on the remaining cells.

Shading problems can be minimized by proper selection of panel location. Of course, the panel must face south but even with this constraint, there are generally several locations where the panels could be placed.

Finding a shade- free location for the solar panel is the key to getting good performance from a solar panel. If you can improve the performance, you get more output per panel and this reduces the number of panels required, so that your costs are reduced.

Unwanted shading can occur due to a variety of obstructions: trees, neighbouring structures, other solar panels, lampposts, electrical poles and transformers. So how do you find out which areas will be shaded and at what time?

One way is to simply observe the shadows in the south facing areas of the house. However, you will need to make observations over an entire year so this is not a very practical method. It is also unnecessary, because a few simple tools will give you this information for the entire year.

You need to determine the path of the sun during the solar window. We have already explained what this is – a window of opportunity when there is adequate sunlight during the day.

Generally, the solar window is between 9 am and 3 p.m. during the day. During this period, the solar array should be free of shade as far as possible. The solar window gets smaller during winter when daylight hours are reduced.

The sun chart is a very useful tool for determining the path of the sun at any given time of the year. As we have already explained, the path is different for different seasons.

Sun charts show the path of the sun for each latitude, for every month of the year. Using these charts, you can determine the position of the sun at any given time of the day at any given time of the year. It is a simple and practical approach but if you want to go more sophisticated, there are also commercially available siting devices with built-in sun charts that show the location of the sun automatically.

Renewable energy consultants use these devices during their site survey. However, you don't have to spend precious dollars in buying one of these devices.

All you really need is a good quality magnetic compass and a protractor and some data about the magnetic declination for your city. For example, if you live in Ottawa, Ontario, the magnetic declination is 6 degrees. This means that the true south is 6 degrees east of the location shown by a magnetic compass.

For Canada, values of declination can readily be calculated for any major city using this simple on-line calculation tool:

http://geomag.nrcan.gc.ca/apps/mdcal-eng.php?Year=2009&Month=10&Day=1&Lat=45&Min=25.5&LatSign=1&Long=75&Min2=42&LongSign=-1&Submit=Calculate+magnetic+declination&CityIndex=212

For example, if you input Ottawa, Ontario into this calculator it immediately gives you the declination as 13° 35' West.

For the US, values of declination can be using a similar calculator from the NOAA web site:

http://www.ngdc.noaa.gov/geomagmodels/Declination.jsp

This calculator requires the zip code of an area in the US, or the latitude and longitude as inputs.

Carry out the following steps to evaluate your site in terms of shading:

1.   Stand at the centre of where you want your solar array to be located. In many cases, this will be some point on your roof. Note: If

you go out on the roof, you must be fully protected with a proper safety devices such as harnesses.

2.   Use your compass to find out the magnetic north and from there, the magnetic south. Correct this reading with the magnetic declination to locate the direction of true south.

3.   Locate the direction of true east, using the compass.

4   In this direction, check for any obstruction. Measure the altitude of the obstruction using the protractor and mark this point on the solar chart.

5.   Rotate 15 degrees to the west and repeat this process by marking any obstructions on the sun chart.

6.   keep repeating this process at 15-degree intervals until you have scanned the entire area up to 90 degrees west. Keep marking the obstruction points on the sun chart.

7.   Now join the obstruction points on the sun chart with a single line.

8.   Shade all the area below this line.

9.   If the site is acceptable, there will be no shading during the solar window i.e. between 9 a.m. and 3 p.m on any day throughout the year.

10.   If the site is not acceptable try a location a few feet to the left or the right, until you fins the site closest to the requirement of zero shading during the solar window.

This process is described in more detail in *Photovoltaics Design & Installation Manual.* See Chapter 11, Useful Resources.

In practice, you will never find a perfect site for your solar installation. Designing is all about making trade-offs and using the existing resources in the best possible way. You may not be able to point the array exactly due south because of various obstructions that cause shading at some time or the other during the year.

As a rule of thumb, if the array is 15 degrees away from true south it will collect 90% of the available energy.

5.5   Sizing Your Panel

Now we come to the real fun stuff that you have all been waiting for – sizing and selecting your solar PV array. Now, you will finally decide what type of solar panels you need and how many of them to buy.

Before you size your solar PV panels, you should estimate the expected efficiency of the system, based on the information gathered so far. We already estimated the efficiency of the system during the planning stage in Chapter 4, but now it is time to refine those calculations a little more. Now that you have more information about where the panels will be installed, you can calculate the efficiency with a much greater degree of precision.

Complete the Table given below, noting down the loss of efficiency for each of the items, listing how much the efficiency departs from the ideal conditions.

Table 5-3: Design Efficiency of Solar PV array

Site location:				
Factor	**Description**	**Best**	**Actual**	**Loss of efficiency**
Tilt Angle				
Orientation				
Shading				
Module temperature				
Other factors				
Total Loss of Efficiency				
Overall efficiency of array				

Most of these factors have been discussed in the previous section; add any other factors that you think will affect the efficiency of the panel.

At this stage, you have a choice to make. You can stick with the original estimates of system capacity that were developed during the planning stage or, you can re-size the system based on the revised estimate for efficiency. It is probably best to stick with the original estimate and accept a slightly reduced performance; at least the cost estimate will not change. However, if you so desire, you can re-size the array using the more refined estimate of the system's efficiency.

Design Capacity Of Panel =Planned capacity/Design Efficiency

Now, you need to select photovoltaic panels that

will produce the required power. For this, you need to know what sizes and capacities of photovoltaic panels are available in the marketplace. This information can never be static; it keeps changing all the time depending upon the latest market conditions.

We do not endorse any manufacturer of renewable energy equipment. The information provided below is purely illustrative and it is provided only for general guidance.

Table 5-4: Solar Panel Sizes and Models					
Make	**Watts**	**Price**	**US $/watt**	**L inch**	**W inch**
Sun	120	$330.00	2.75	59	27
Evergreen	195	$487.00	2.50	65	37
Cansolar	200	No data			
Sharp	80	$365.00	4.56	47	21
Sharp	123	$579.00	4.71		
	175	$699.00	3.99	62	32.5
	198	$879.00	4.44		
	216	$899.00	4.16		
Kyocera	135	$549.00	4.07	59	26
	210	$849.00	4.04		
Sanyo	195	$999.00	5.12		

Note: This data is current only at the time of writing (2009). The information, especially the pricing part, is subject to change. The information is presented only to help in designing; users must verify the information from the primary sources when they do the actual design. Prices are in US dollars.

You can now begin selecting the photovoltaic panel

that best meets your requirement. The elements to look out for are:

> ➤ A reputed make
> ➤ Low price per watt
> ➤ High output per unit weight
> ➤ High output per unit area

The 175 watt panel seems to meet most of this requirement. We will use this panel just to illustrate the sizing process; it is definitely not an endorsement of this particular product.

Next, you need to decide on how many panels you need. This is simply calculated as:

N = DC*1000/Out
>   Where N = number of panels
>   DC=Design Capacity, KW
>   Out =Output per panel, Watts

Thus, if you need to produce 1 KW of solar power, you will need:

N = 1000/175 = 5.7 panels.

This would be rounded off to 6 panels.

We can now apply this technique to our sample project.

Exercise 5-1:Solar Panel Selection

Sample Project: Located in Ottawa, Ontario
Objective: To select the solar panels
Analysis
Capacity of Project = 1.55 KW, from Planning stage

Factor	Actual	Optimum	Loss efficiency
Tilt Angle	40 degrees, mounting on existing roof	45 degrees for this location	5%
Orientation	Due South	Due South	0%
Shade	Some trees in solar path	No shading	10%
Temperature	Ottawa is a cold climate	Cold climate	0%
Total Loss of Eff.			15%
eff. of array			85%

If we want the same performance as in the planning stage, the revised Design Capacity = 1.55/0.85 =1.82 KW
However, we decide to stay with the original capacity, to keep costs under control.
A good choice for solar panel appears to be the 175

watt model.

Hence, Number of modules = 1.55*1000/175 = 6.2

Rounding this off, we need 7 modules

Results

We need 7　　modules of 175 watt each for this project.

5.6　Panel Mounting Options

There are a number of different ways that you can install the solar PV panels, as listed below:

Pole Mount

You might decide to install the solar panels in your backyard, if you have the space available and if shading is not an issue. If you make this choice, consider using pole-mounted solar arrays.

Pole mounting offers the following advantages:

- ✓ Easy installation
- ✓ The orientation of the panels is easily adjusted
- ✓ The tilt angle is also adjustable
- ✓ Tracking systems can be used

Hence, with a pole-mounted installation, you can easily optimize the array for maximum efficiency.

There are several different options for pole mounting: side-of-pole mounting, front-of-the pole mounting and above the pole mounting. Tracking systems can readily be built in to any of these options. As a homeowner, you may not, however, want the added complexity and cost of a tracking system.

The method works best for ground level installations. There could, however, be theft issues with a ground mounted solar photovoltaic system.

Flush Mounts

Flush mounting is a simple and economical method of mounting the solar panels on the roof. They generally consist of nothing more than end brackets or "Z" brackets that mount to the panel frame and then screw or bolt into the roof. Flush Mounts are typically used with small solar arrays on rooftops, generally when installing only one or two panels. The structural design of a flush mount cannot support a larger number of solar panels.

When installing a flush mount with your solar panel, ensure that there is adequate clearance between the surface of the roof and the underside of the photovoltaic panel. The clearance should be at least 50-100 mm. This clearance is essential for allowing airflow under the panel to keep it cool. If you do not provide adequate clearance, the photovoltaic unit will heat up, reducing both operating efficiency and equipment life.

With a flush mounting system, the orientation and the tilt angle of the solar array is fixed; it cannot be adjusted for the time of the year.

Direct mounts

This is another simple method of mounting solar

panels directly on the roof.

With this approach, the panels rest directly on over the roof tiles, held in place by suitable supports. It is a low cost method but there is no control over the tilt angle; it has to be the same as the roof slope.

The main drawback to this type of mounting is the lack of clearance between the roof and the underside of the panel. Since there is no air gap, the panels can easily overheat causing loss of efficiency and reduced equipment life.

<u>Frame mounts</u>

The panel is mounted over a metal frame that allows some control over tilt angle, so it can be better matched to the design requirements. The metal frame is fixed to the roof using suitable supports. The frame could be as simple as a set of track below the solar panels.

The main disadvantage is the extra cost and the extra weight of the mounting frame.

5.7 Inverter Selection

Before selecting the inverter, there are a couple of decisions to be made. Until very recently, there was only one choice: selecting an inverter sized to match the output from the photovoltaic panel array. In other words, there was only one inverter for a number of photovoltaic panels. This remains, no doubt, the most economical approach.

However, in recent times, some manufacturers have introduced new designs where an inverter is provided for each photovoltaic module. If your design uses three PV modules, for example, then there will be three inverters. The benefit of this approach is scalability. The project can be scaled up at any time; you can add more PV modules as required. In this case, the PV module manufacturer sizes the inverters for you as the PV module and the inverter are sold as a package.

This approach may be very attractive to some people who do not want to go for a full-scale project all at once. However, you must examine its drawbacks carefully. With more inverters, there will be more high voltage wiring required. Also, the inverters will be on the roof, adding to weight issues. Of course, if you go with this approach, you can avoid the inverter sizing exercise that follows.

Before you select inverters, it is helpful to have some basic understanding of how these devices function. Essentially, they simply convert a low voltage dc signal to a high voltage ac output that is compatible with the grid frequency. Hence, the inverter forms the interface between your solar PV array and the grid.

There are basically two types of inverters used in solar photovoltaic applications. The first type is the stand-alone or static inverter. These are used primarily in off the grid applications where the solar photovoltaic panels are used to supply the home's electricity needs directly. They provide an AC output but the frequency and the phase will not necessarily be an exact match with the grid conditions.

The other type of inverters is used for connecting to the power grid. These are called line-tied inverters or, more usually, grid- intertie inverters. This is a more demanding application, since the utilities have much more stringent requirements for the quality of the power supplied to them. The most important requirement is that the inverter output frequency and phase angle must be synchronized with the grid power frequency and phase angle. Hence these devices are also referred to as synchronous inverters.

If you don't know what a phase angle is, don't worry about. It is a technical term that relates to the quality of the power. You don't have to know what it is – the inverter designer should have the required knowledge.

This book deals largely with solar photovoltaic systems connected to the grid, because if you don't connect to the grid, you will not get the benefits of generous incentive programs such as Feed-in Tariffs. Hence, we will talk only about grid-intertie type inverters here.

To size the inverter correctly, simply match the inverter rating, in watts or kilowatts, to the design output of the solar photovoltaic system, keeping a margin of at least 20%. In other words, the inverter must be over sized by at least 20%. If you plan on a future expansion, it might be prudent to use an even larger inverter capacity.

Known manufacturers of inverters include Fronius,

Beacon, Xantrex and Outback. A typical grid-tie inverter rated at 2500 Watts is priced at around $1550.00, at the time of writing. A 5300-watt unit costs about $3,050.00. As you can see from this, it is a fairly expensive part of the solar photovoltaic system and there are economies of scale to be had in using a larger system.

If you do your project in stages, putting in a few photovoltaic panels at a time, you could end up spending more money on inverters. It might be helpful to plan the entire project at once and to buy components like inverters and disconnects sized for the entire project. Then you could buy the photovoltaic panels in stages, as needed.

Many grid-tie inverters come equipped with built-in disconnect switches so it might be possible to eliminate a separate disconnect switch. However, you will have to check this out with the local authorities if they will accept built-in disconnects.

The inverter that you select must be rated for outdoor use.

Exercise 5-2: Inverter Selection

Sample Project: Located in Ottawa, Ontario
Objective: To select the inverter
Analysis
Capacity of Project = 1.55 KW
To allow for future expansion, a higher capacity of at least 2 KW is required.
Result
Grid-intertie inverter, capacity 2000 Watts.

5.8 Disconnect Switch Selection

The disconnect switch is connected between the inverter and the point at which the solar photovoltaic system is connected to the grid. Disconnect switches are rated in terms of amperage and voltage rating i.e. 30 amps, 240 VAC.

Your disconnect switch should have at least a 50% higher rating than the inverter. For example, if the inverter is rated at 2500 watts, select a disconnect switch with a rating of 30 amps, 240 volts. This can handle up to about 6000 watts of power.

Known manufactures of disconnect switches include Square D.

If you break your project up into stages, size your disconnect switch for the complete project; the cost does not vary too much with the size of the switch. It is advantageous to go with excess capacity right from the beginning.

Exercise 5-3:Disconnect switch Selection

Sample Project: Located in Ottawa, Ontario
Objective: To select the disconnect switch
Analysis
Capacity of Project = 1.55 KW
To allow for future expansion, a higher capacity of at least 3 KW is required.
Result
Disconnect, capacity 3KW. Rating 15 amps, 240V

5.9 Wiring Selection

For selection of wiring and conduit, consider the two types of circuits that are involved:

1. Low voltage DC wiring, between the solar PV modules and the inverter.
2. Line voltage AC wiring, between the inverter and the disconnect switch.

The low voltage DC wiring is mostly outside the house and must be located inside a weatherproof conduit. It must meet the requirements of all applicable code and standards.

In general, solar photovoltaic system wiring must comply with the requirements of the National Electric Code to ensure that the system is safe and functional. This book will not attempt to describe all the requirements of this code but will only highlight some important requirements. In most jurisdictions, local electrical codes will also apply.

So, why do we talk about the NEC in this book? It is simply because many local electrical codes are derived from the NEC so if you understand what the NEC is all about, you will better appreciate what is needed for a solar photovoltaic system.

Direct current systems are quite different from AC systems and they run at a much lower voltage. DC wiring tends to be a size larger than AC wiring carrying the same current. AC and DC wiring systems are not compatible with each other and one should never be substituted for the other.

There are a number of wire types in use in power systems. The material itself may be either copper or aluminium. As you probably know from Electricity 101, copper has a much higher conductivity and is widely used in residential wiring. Aluminium has lower conductivity but being lighter, it is often used in high voltage transmission lines. Because it is brittle and less durable, the NEC for interior home wiring does not permit the use of Aluminium.

The wiring used in the home is covered by insulation that provides protection against heat, abrasion, moisture and ultra-violet light. The NEC indicates what types of insulated wire can be used for various applications; there are categories for dry, indoor locations, for indoor/outdoor locations and for underground locations. All wiring exposed to sunlight must be labelled "Sunlight resistant".

Two or more insulated wires can be put inside an overall covering, called a cable. The NEC specifies the types of covering can be used for different locations. For example, type NMC can be used in moist locations such as laundry rooms; type NM is permitted only for dry, indoor locations. All cables exposed to sunlight must be labelled as "sunlight resistant".

A conduit is a plastic or metal pipe that offers a protective enclosure for wires. Conduits are used very often in photovoltaic systems since the wiring is exposed to weather conditions. Conduits are also good for concealing wiring runs. The wiring from inside the photovoltaic panel generally connects to junction boxes. Single conductors are then passed through the junction boxes to make the electrical connections. For example, if several PV panels need to be connected together in an electric circuit, conduits will be used between the junction boxes. Very often, rigid PVC pipes are used as conduits.

Sizing of electric wires is done on the basis of wire gauge, ampacity and voltage drop. The wire gauge is indicated as American Wire Gauge (AWG) size. These numbers work in reverse; the smaller the AWG wire size, the more current it can carry safely.

Ampacity is the current carrying ability of the wire, expressed in amperes. Going back to Electricity 101, the larger the current in a wire, the hotter it will get. Hence, electrical codes such as NEC limit how much current is allowed for a given AWG size. This information is given in Ampacity tables.

To size the wire in a photovoltaic system by ampacity, find out the highest current load for the given circuit. If you are looking at the wire run from the solar array to the inverter, use the short circuit current for each panel multiplied by the number of panels. This is because the panels are connected in parallel, as shown in the figure below. To find out the short circuit current, look at the specification sheet for that photovoltaic panel.

A margin of safety is also required; hence multiply this current by 125%, to ensure that the wiring never carries more than 80% of the current. This safety factor is required by Code on all wiring runs in the PV system.

Once the current is determined, the wire size can be determined from tables, such as Table 9-4 in the

National Electric Code.

For example, if there are five PV panels in an array and the short circuit current is eight amperes, the total short circuit current is (5*8) or, 40 amperes. The margin of safety is 125%. Hence the ampacity is 50 amperes. Using NEC, this leads to the selection of AWG 6 wire Type UF, AWN in conduit.

Once the wire gauge has been selected based on its current carrying capacity, you must consider the acceptable limits of the voltage drop in the wiring. These limits depend upon the length of the wire. In general, the voltage drop must be less than 2-5% of the total voltage in that system. This limits the length of the wire that can be used.

Increasing the wire size can reduce the voltage drop. So, if the voltage drop is too high, choose the next larger wire size (i.e. next smaller AWG number) and repeat the calculation for the Ampacity. It may take iteration or two to get acceptable results.

Ensure that the sizing exercise is carried out for each wire in the solar photovoltaic system.

In addition to wiring, the electrical system must provide for circuit breakers and overload protection. All of these elements must conform to the National Electric Code.

The process of selecting wires according to the NEC is described in detail in the *Photovoltaics Design & Installation Manual.* See Chapter 11,

Useful Resources.

> **It is strongly recommended that a qualified electrician should prepare or verify the electrical wiring design to ensure that it complies with applicable codes**

5.10   Other Accessories

Ensure that all other accessories required for the project are selected. These could include:

Lightning arrestors
Overcurrent protectors
Junction boxes
Cable glands
Panel mounting hardware
Miscellaneous hardware

Consult with the electrical contractor before finalizing these details.

5.11   Prepare Schematics

Schematics may be required for submission to approval authorities. They are also essential for proper design of the solar photovoltaic system.

The schematics should indicate the locations of the major components such as the photovoltaic panels. They should where these panels are placed on the roof and how they are mounted. You can provide mounting details that show precisely how the components fit together. The schematics should also show where components such as inverters, disconnect switches and fuses are located.

For small home projects, the schematics may be hand sketches or drawn using a simple drafting program. My own preference is for making the sketches using Visio, which is simpler to use than other CAD programs such as Autocad.

Also, wiring diagrams are required for each circuit. To prepare wiring diagrams correctly, you need a basic knowledge of AC and DC circuits. Also, you need to know about series and parallel circuits and how they are used.

In general, the individual cells are connected in series inside the solar photovoltaic panels. This means that if one cell breaks down, the entire circuit could be broken causing zero output from that panel. Normally, this is avoided by providing diode protection. Diodes, as you may recall from Electricity 101, allow current flow in only one direction. By providing a protective diode, a defective cell can be by-passed.

Generally, the photovoltaic panels are connected in parallel; the output from each panel goes to a combiner box that feeds into the inverter.

The installer or the energy consultant may also prepare the schematics, but it is helpful for the homeowner to prepare hand sketches that can be developed further, if required. The homeowner should also prepare some preliminary circuit diagrams that can be refined further by the electrician or a professional consultant.

5.12 Prepare Bill of Materials

A bill of materials is a listing of the material required for completing the project, presented in a standard format. It could be on a simple spreadsheet, or sometimes, written directly on the drawing. The spreadsheet format is the best, as it can be expanded to include costs, ordering information etc. It also specifies some details about the equipment. It should contain the following information.

1. Name of material - for example, solar PV panel.
2. Brief description – for example- "polycrystalline photovoltaic panel"
3. Approximate dimensions
4. Manufacturer
5. Manufacturer's part number
6. Essential specifications, in summary format
7. Quantity required
8. Cost of each component
9. Total cost of all material

The bill of materials can also be inserted into one of the schematic drawings, using the copy and paste command.

Along with the Bill of Materials, compile the specification sheets for each component in hard copy format. Then you can place all the items in a project file folder. The tech savvy, may, however, prefer to keep only electronic records; just make sure you have back-ups on a DVD or a CD. Keeping good records is essential for the success of your project.

5.13 Verify all details

Once the project is fully defined, it is necessary to verify each and every detail. Check all the calculations, verify site conditions once again, and make sure everything will work as intended. Check the rate of return calculations again, this time using the information collected in the design stage. Use the exact costs of the equipment and installation as fast as possible.

Make sure, once again, that the project complies with all applicable regulations, the building code and all safety standards. At this stage, it is worthwhile to take the plans to the local hydro company, the municipal authorities or any other concerned regulatory authority. Have discussions with the officials; most of them are helpful and will give useful advice.

You should also talk to the installation company that you intend too use. Based on these consultations, modify the calculations, schematics and bill of materials as required.

5.14 Solar PV Kits

Some manufacturers also offer ready-to-use solar photovoltaic kits. They can be useful for beginners as they ensure that all required components are included and that they have been correctly sized. However, you have to complete the planning process and much of the design phase before you know enough to order one of these kits. Essentially, you need to know what is the design capacity of the solar photovoltaic system that you need. You cannot bypass the critical planning and design steps and still hope to get a good product.

It is worthwhile to go through the design exercise, so you can cost the system component by component. After this exercise, you can compare the prices with a ready-to-use kit and see if you are getting a good deal or not.

Typically, a ready-to-use kit will include the following items;

Solar panels
Inverters
Electrical components such as boxes and cabling
Disconnects

The kit should also come with line diagrams that will make the approval and installation process a little easier.

However, even if you buy a kit, you are still responsible for getting all the permits and approvals and making sure that everything works correctly. Hence, even if you decide to buy a kit, you still have to go through the design process and make sure all components meet your requirements. Also, each home is different and you will have to check if the standard components in the kit will meet your individual needs.

For example, you still need to find out where the

solar panels will be installed and whether there is enough space available for the installation. Also, you have to look at the shading problems on your rooftop and check if a standard kit can successfully address those problems.

You may also have to meet local content requirements; it is little easier to do so if some of the hardware is sourced from a local supplier. One approach would be use the information provided in the specifications for the kit, and buy locally to the maximum extent possible. There is also the risk factor – if the system does not work as well as intended, it is harder to get help from a distant supplier. The risk is a little less if you take help from your friendly, neighbourhood supplier of solar photovoltaic equipment.

Chapter 6: Lining Up Your Permits

Contents

6.1 The Approval Process
6.2 The Building Permit Folks
6.3 Getting Past the Ontario Power Authority
6.4 Satisfying the Electrical Safety Authority
6.5 Applying for the Utility Connection

Installation of Roof-mounted Solar Panels
Courtesy: The Renewable Energy Laboratory, US Department of Energy

6.1   The Approval Process

By this time, you have completed the design of your solar photovoltaic system. You know the sizes, capacities and quantities of the solar photovoltaic panels needed for your project. You know exactly where to mount them and you have a fairly accurate idea of how much renewable energy the system will generate. You have selected all the other electrical hardware required for the project, including the inverter, the disconnect switch, safety devices and wiring for all the circuits. However, you haven't spent real money on the project because you haven't bought any equipment yet.

Before you go out on a spending spree, you must get all required permits and clearances for the project. You will not be allowed to connect to the grid until all your approvals are in place, including final approval by the Electrical Safety Authority.

Don't be daunted by the approval process; it is far simpler than it appears at first glance. True, there are a number of players involved but you will not run into too many problems if you have followed a systematic approach to planning and design, as indicated in this book.

And, remember, there is always plenty of help available en route. This book is a good guidepost and there is plenty of good information out there on the web, too. Make sure you research the web sites of each of the approval agencies that are involved for your project.

To get you started, here is a brief checklist of the approval agencies who may be involved in your project. Remember, you may not need all the approvals; for examples, a change in building permit may not be required for your project. Also, there are regional variations as each province and territory can set its own rules.

Note: The information in Table 6-1 has been compiled mainly for Ontario.

Table 6-1: The Approval Process			
Authority	**Type of Approval**	**Approx. Time Frame**	**Comment**
Ontario Power Authority	For getting approval of Feed In Tariff or Net Metering	30 days	Requires full info about the project
Utility Company	For connecting to utility grid	Two weeks After ESA	
Local Municipality	For changes to building permit	Two weeks	
Environmental Agency	Environmental clearance	Varies	Not required for solar PV systems
Electrical Safety Authority	Inspection of electrical installation	Two weeks	Approval required

6.2 *The Building Permit Folks*

You must have obtained a building permit from the local municipal authority when your house was built. If you bought a pre-owned house, you just might have to dig out a copy from the municipal office. It might, however, been filed with the building inspection report as most people get the house inspected before finalizing the sale.

An amendment to the permit may be required for an alteration such as adding solar panels to the roof. Just check with your local municipal office; if you are lucky, the existing building permit will still be valid.

Don't worry – all that the building permit folks are looking for is that the health and safety of the occupants is not compromised in any way. For this, they may want to verify if the roof can support the weight of the solar array, as this is the biggest safety concern.

If you have followed the design procedures laid out in the previous chapter, there should not be a problem. So have a word with the building inspector and, if required, submit a copy of the plans for the renewal energy project to the building code department for approval.

6.3   Getting Past the OPA

Power authorities, such as the Ontario Power Authority are a little more demanding; they have more at stake as they have the ultimate responsibility for creating and managing the Feed-in Tariff program. Also, they are responsible for planning upgrades to the grid infrastructure to ensure it meets all future needs. Each time the OPA approves an application for a renewable energy project, it has to make sure there is enough capacity in the power grid system to meet the additional load. Hence the OPA will scrutinize every application very carefully to see if it meets all their requirements.

The Ontario Power Authority has developed a special Feed-in Tariff Program tailored towards homeowners and small businesses. This program uses a simpler application process. It is called the micro FIT program and applies to projects smaller than 10kW capacity. The program is described in detail in the OPA website at:

http://microfit.powerauthority.on.ca/

Since the program is described in detail in the very informative OPA website, we will only touch on a few highlights so you can get a feel for how the program works.

The micro FIT program offers several options for participation. The participants could simply own their projects; this is probably the simplest option and the one that most homeowners would prefer.

However, you can, if you like, lease your property to a renewable energy developer. This means, effectively, that if you have a large rooftop, you could rent it out to a developer.

You can either buy the equipment needed for your project, or lease it from a supplier. You can also set up a project with others in your locality. So, if you live in a townhouse or a single-family home, you could, potentially, convince your neighbours to join hands for community renewal energy project.

Project Eligibility Requirements

* ❖ The project must be located in Ontario
* ❖ The project must use solar photovoltaic systems, wind power, water power, biomass, biogas or landfill gas
* ❖ Projects must meet Ontario content requirements, currently set at minimum 40%
* ❖ Projects must connect to a distribution system; there must be no prior OPA contract in place and separate metering must be provided
* ❖ Projects must be 10 KW or less

You can also apply for an expansion of an existing project in one of the eligible categories as long as the total capacity remains less than 10KW.

The Application Process

There are a few important steps to be followed during the application process.

Step 1: Use your legal name for the application

You have several options for the choice of the legal name; the simplest is to apply for the micro FIT program under your own name. If you have a high taxable income, any money you earn through the Feed in Tariff program could, potentially, be subject to taxation.

If your spouse or significant other has a lower income, consider using that name for the application; you might need to consult a tax advisor first.

You could also set up a separate business entity and apply under that name; this might be very useful as you can charge depreciation on the assets and also write off some business expenses.

You may also decide to set up a community project. If you live in a town home, quite possibly there will be a row of town homes on your street. If they all have adequate number of south-facing roofs, it might be an excellent idea to join hands and start a community project. This will reduce the equipment costs as you get the economy of scale. However, the legal implications should be explored fully before you take this step.

Step 2: Download a sample application form.

The actual application for the micro FIT project is done on line. However, it is good to work with a hard copy until you have assembled all the required information.

A sample application form can also be downloaded from the OPA web-site at:

http://microfit.powerauthority.on.ca/pdf/microFIT-Application-Form-Sample.pdf

Step 3: Fill in Section 1: general information.

In this section provide general information such as

legal name, type of project, location, contact information, type of applicant, GST registration number, if any.

Step 4: Complete Section 2: Eligibility requirements

Fill in the details that demonstrate that you are eligible for the project and that you have no existing contract with OPA that could disqualify you. Provide details of your existing utility account. Also, indicate if you want to convert an existing Net Metering account to the micro FIT program or if you plan an incremental expansion of an existing program.

Indicate the type of your project i.e. solar photovoltaic, wind energy, etc. and its proposed capacity. Also, provide information about any additional sources of funding for the project. You must also indicate if you will provide a battery back-up system.

Finally, give a brief description of this project, including the relevant design details. Note that the OPA application form does not ask for schematics and wiring diagrams; those details may, however, be required by other approval agencies such as the Electrical Safety Authority.

Step 5: Complete Section 3: Declaration

In this section, you basically tick mark the three check boxes. You state that the information submitted to OPA is correct and you authorize OPA and your utility company to collect any additional information that they need in connection with the micro FIT program.

You also declare that you understand the domestic content requirements that are an essential eligibility requirement for this program.

Step 6: Wait for OPA response

OPA will acknowledge receipt of your application with a form letter and if the application is accepted, you will get a contract offer within thirty days. You must accept this offer within one year.

Once you have this contract in place, you are free to approach the utility company with a connection request.

6.4   Satisfying the ESA

The Electrical Safety Authority (ESA) decides if your renewable energy installation is safe enough to be connected to the power grid. As stated in its website, the ESA believes that any system that produces even small amounts of electricity is potentially dangerous. Also, you will not get permission to connect to the power grid until ESA gives its stamp of approval.

The ESA has produced a 16-page booklet geared especially towards small producers of renewable energy or, in their lingo, towards Micro-embedded generation projects. You can download this booklet from:

http://esasafe.com/pdf/Micro_Embedded_Generation_Facilities_Guidelines.pdf

The ESA guidelines are based, essentially on the Ontario Electrical Safety Code and the Ontario Energy Board's Electrical Distribution Code.

The ESA does not recommend doing your own electrical work. However, if you feel you are competent enough to do so, you must submit an "Application for Inspection" to the ESA.

In fact, the ESA recommends that a qualified electrical contractor or electrician should do all electrical work for a renewal energy project, as this type of work is beyond the ability of most do-it-yourselfers. The ESA also recommends checking if any local by-laws or permits apply to this type of installation.

Once this checking has been done, the ESA recommends that you should apply to the Local Distribution Company (i.e. the local utility company) for permission to install the renewable energy system. After obtaining this approval, select a qualified electrical contractor; the booklet lists the requirements that the electrical contractor should meet. The contractor will file the Application for Inspection with the ESA once the electrical work has been completed.

After this occurs, the ESA will send its electrical inspector to the site. If the inspection is satisfactory, the ESA will issue a "Connection Authorization" to the utility company and provide a Certificate of Inspection to the electrical contractor. Once this has been done, you can approach the utility company and finalize the connection agreement.

The Inspection Process

The inspection process is very thorough. Each piece of equipment must be properly labelled and meet all required standards. Refer to the ESA guideline for details.

6.5   Applying for Utility Connection

The utility companies allow renewable energy producers to connect to the utility grid, but the renewable energy producers retain the responsible for the safety of the installation and for the cost of connection to the grid.

You must complete the application form that can be downloaded from the utility company's web site; Ottawa residents can use the following link:

http://www.hydroottawa.com/pdfs/specs/Appendix E.pdf

Residents in other areas must go to their local utility companies' website, or contact the utility company directly.

The utility application form will be a piece of cake for you, because, by this time you are used to completing much more complex documents. The application form asks for basic information about you and your project and, of course, clearance from the Electrical Safety Authority.

Chapter 7: Installing the Project

Contents
7.1   Ordering the Equipment
7.2   Testing the Equipment
7.3   Installing the Roof-top panels
7.4   Installing the Electrical System
7.5   Starting the System

Installing a Solar Array
Courtesy:National Renewable Energy Laboratory, US Department of Energy

7.1 Ordering the Equipment

By this time, you have successfully planned your project to get a good idea of what you need, how much it will cost and how the project will benefit you. You have also completed the design development phase, where you have ironed out all the pesky design details and you have working sketches, schematics and full specifications of what you are buying. You have also refined your cost estimates and your expectations for the return on your investment. You also have necessary permits and approvals.

However, so far, all you have to show for your work is paperwork. Now it is time to convert your dreams into reality.

Start by ordering the equipment from the Bill of Materials that you prepared at the conclusion of the development of design phase. You can order all the components at once, to save shipping, handling and overhead costs. Allow about three week for shipment; it could, however, vary from manufacturer to manufacturer.

Or, you might take a more prudent approach and order the material in bits and pieces. You could order one solar photovoltaic panel, the inverter, the disconnect switch, wiring and the safety devices. After you test out one panel and it works to your satisfaction, you can order the rest of the equipment. The choice is yours. Of course, if you order a complete solar photovoltaic kit, then you will get all the equipment at once.

Regardless of which approach you follow, you need a systematic test procedure. You must test each component individually, and then test the completed system, perhaps assembled in your backyard. Once each component and the complete system pass all the tests, you are ready for the final installation. After final installation, test the complete system once more, before connecting to the utility grid. This systematic approach will save you time, money and headaches.

Plus, it's a lot more fun this way as you get to play with your toys.

7.2   Testing the Equipment

This may well be the most exciting part of the project, for those who have never installed a solar photovoltaic system before. Unpack the panels and read the manufacturer's instructions very carefully. Then, assemble the panel in your backyard and improvise some temporary supports to match, as closely as possible, the tilt angle of the actual installation. Orient the panel exactly in the same direction as you would in the final installation.

Then test the open circuit voltage i.e. the voltage produced when nothing is connected to the panel. For this, all you really need is a good quality digital multi-meter. Note down the open voltage reading along with the date of the observation.

After this, test the short-circuit current; this is the current that flows through the panel when there is no load in the output circuit. You can perform this test, also, using a digital multi-meter.

This test should not damage the solar panel, because it has a sizable internal resistance that will limit the current to the short-circuit value indicated in the manufacturer's specifications. It is not like shorting the terminals of a battery, where the output current can go out of control. However, keep the short-circuit current test as brief as possible, not more than a few seconds.

Also, visually inspect the panel for any sign of damage and check that the module is attached securely to the mounting brackets. Check for any damaged junction boxes or loose wires. Check the insulation using a digital multi-meter; it should show open circuit, i.e. infinite resistance reading.

The panel should be clearly labelled, in accordance with Code requirements. The terminals should be clearly marked as positive or negative. The maximum over current rating should be indicated, as also the open-circuit voltage, operating current, short-circuit current, etc. Record all your observations in a tabular format. Repeat the test for each solar photovoltaic panel and maintain complete records.

Once all the panels have been tested, wire them together using the combiner box, and repeat similar tests for the combined output. Once you are satisfied that the panels work well together, make a temporary connection to the inverter and the disconnect switch to test this portion of the system.

Check the output from the inverter and ensure that

the disconnect switch and all safety devices are working correctly.

Once you are done with the testing, you are ready to proceed with the actual installation

7.3 Installing the Roof- top Panels

Roof top installation is dangerous work. It may look easy but there have been far too many accidents in homes when doing roof work.

We strongly recommend calling a professional installer for all roof work!

Only the most experienced, handy man type homeowners should attempt this work themselves. If you do decide to do this yourself (WE DO NOT RECOMMEND THIS), make sure you use all the safety gear including helmets and harnesses.

Install the panels strictly according to the manufacturer's instructions. If you are doing rack mounting, a metal framework will be bolted to the roofs' structural members and the panels will be installed on top of this frame. Keep an air gap between the roof and the panels as air circulation will help keep the panels cool.

If you do direct or flush mounting, the panels will be fixed directly to the roof using special clamps and fixtures. The panels will run at appreciably higher temperatures but there will be less weight on the roof. Make sure that the integrity of the roof structure is maintained so that there is no possibility of leakage.

Even if you call in a professional installer, make sure the panels are mounted securely and that the roof remains completely weather tight.

7.4 Installing the electrical equipment

Again, our advice is simple.

CALL IN A CERTIFIED ELECTRICIAN.

There are many reasons for this piece of advice.

1. Low voltage wiring on the roof is difficult and dangerous.
2. High voltage wiring is intrinsically dangerous.
3. All electrical wiring will be subject to inspection by the Electrical Safety Authority; it is much easier to get approval if the wiring is done professionally
4. The electrician will verify the design and make sure all the safety devices are in place and that they function correctly.

To find a certified electrician, you can often use the resources listed in the Electrical safety Authority web site. For Ontario, use the following web site:

http://www.esasafe.com/GeneralPublic/hc_003.php?s=8

If you live outside Ontario, check with the local electrical safety authority to locate a certified electrician. If you already have an electrician on your list, make sure this person is approved and authorized to apply for safety inspections on your behalf.

7.5 Starting the system

Now that everything is connected, you can start the system, preferably in the presence of the electrician who did the installation. First, keep the disconnect switch off and test the entire system. Once the testing is complete, you may need to call in the inspector from the utility company to verify that everything is perfectly safe. After this, you will be connected to the utility grid.

After this, you can relax and watch the electricity savings roll in, year after year.

Chapter 8: Other Renewable Energy Projects

Contents

8.1   Introduction
8.2   Solar Heating
8.3   Wind Power
8.4   Water Power

Solar Hot Water Heater Installation
Courtesy:National Renewable Energy Laboratory,US Department of Energy

8.1   Introduction

There are quite a few other renewable energy projects that can help you reduce your dependence on conventional energy sources. But as you might have figured out by now, our preference is for solar photovoltaic projects. Photovoltaic systems are clean, easy to install and there are no maintenance hassles.

Plus, with the excellent incentive programs offered by some province such as Ontario, you can make good money out of solar photo-voltaics. It is a little harder to make money out of the other renewal energy projects.

However, there are special situation where you might want to install other types of renewable energy systems. If you live in a remote farm or cottage, you might consider a solar heating system. If you live in a large farm far away from the city, wind power could be very attractive for you.

If you have a stream, river or waterfall on your property, consider a micro-hydro electric project. Many new homes are being built using geothermal energy as a renewable energy source; there might even be some applications for existing homes.

In the following sections, we describe some of these technologies, so that you can decide if they are appropriate for you. However, do note that many of these systems are not so easy to implement and you might have to call in professional help to custom design a system that works best for you.

Also, incentive programs are not very attractive for some of these technologies when you apply them in the home. As an example, Ontario's Feed in Tariff for wind energy is just 15 cents/KWH; this may be appropriate for commercial wind farms, but it is not very attractive for homeowners who do not have the benefits of large-scale production.

This chapter describes the various systems very briefly; for more detailed information, refer to *The Homeowner's Guide to Renewable Energy*. See Chapter 11, Useful Resources.

8.2 Solar Heating

Solar heating has been around since time immemorial. In fact, most homes use some form of passive solar heating. Architects in many homes make generous use of south-facing walls, roofs and windows. Proper architectural design can reduce the home's heating and cooling load very significantly.

However, in this section we will talk about more active systems that produce hot water from solar energy. There are a wide variety of products available in the solar heating marketplace.

Solar Batch Heater

This is the simplest of all solar heating systems and it is very popular in warm countries like Mexico. In its most elementary form, it consists of a water tank placed on the roof of a home. It absorbs heat from the sun during the day time to provide hot water for the home.

Sometimes, the tank is painted black to improve heat absorption. It is a simple system with no moving parts at all. However, it does not work too well in cold climates where the temperature falls below freezing point.

In many cities in India, the municipal water supply is so erratic that many homeowners install a water storage tank on the roof. Most homes in India have two water faucets, one for the fresh water and another for the stored water. During the daytime, the stored water can provide hot water for domestic use.

The problem with this type of system is that, most of the time; it provides hot water at times when you don't really need it. There is a plentiful supply of hot water in the summer afternoons when there is hardly any use for it. The system does not work so well during the cold winter mornings when you really need the hot water. So, the system is, at best, a supplement to a conventional hot water system using gas or electricity.

An improved version of the solar batch heater consists of a large water tank inside a solar collector. This is also referred to as the Integrated Collector & Storage system. Such devices are often used to pre-heat the water that is supplied to a conventional water heater system.

Systems with Separate Collection & Storage

Most commercially available solar hot water systems fall into this category. In these systems, the solar collector is mounted on the roof and there are plumbing connections to a solar hot water storage tank located inside the building.

There are a number of variations of this basic system. Some use a flat plate collector, which consists essentially of heating coils located inside a flat, transparent surface exposed to the sun. Cold water flows into the collector, gets heated and flows out; a number of these collectors may be connected together.

A more advanced system uses evacuated tube collectors, with a higher collection efficiency but using the essentially the same principle.

Thermo siphon System

There are number of different options for feeding the heated water to hot water storage. In the thermo-siphon system, there is no pump. Convection currents are used to drive the flow of water.

So, how does this play out?

When water is heated, its density falls. Hence, hot water tends to rise upwards and this is known as convection. In the thermo siphon system, the hot water storage tank is located a few feet above the solar collector. Hot water rises by convection and collects in the storage tank; cold water is fed to the base of the collector from the hot water tank. As a result of this continuous movement of hot and cold water, the storage tank collects hot water that is now used to supply the home's hot water needs.

It is a pretty cool system, as no pumps are required.

However, it works only for a small hot water demand because as soon as you try to draw more water, it will get cold. Hence, more advanced systems use a pump for the water circulation.

Pumped Hot Water System

Most of these systems use small AC pumps that are operated from the household electricity system. If you want to be totally off the grid, you could, however, use a DC pump driven by power from a solar photovoltaic panel.

In a pumped system, the solar collector can be quite far from the storage tank; the collector could be mounted on the roof or on the ground, depending upon site conditions.

Antifreeze systems

Still more advanced systems use a secondary heat transfer fluid such as propylene glycol. The heat transfer fluid flows through the collector, where it absorbs heat from the sun and this heat is rejected in a heat exchanger. The heat exchanger then transfers the heat to a hot water system. Why do we need such a complicated system? The answer is simple – for freeze-up protection, much like the anti-freeze solution in a car.

The parts of the solar collector system that are exposed to the weather are filled with propylene glycol, which has a very low freezing point. Thus, these parts are protected against freezing in the winter months. The parts of the system that are inside the house do not need this protection and they can use water as the working fluid.

System Selection

With so many available options, you might be wondering which system is best for you. It all depends on the site conditions and on what you want from the system.

In warm climates, the batch heating system is a good, economical solution, if you are willing to supplement solar heating with electric or gas hot water system.

In a colder climate, the thermo-siphon system may work, but only for small sizes. For larger capacities, you need to add a pump.

For very cold climates consider using a system with anti-freeze protection i.e. a system using a secondary heat transfer system. Again, you will probably need a conventional hot water system using gas or electricity as a back up.

You must also consider the fact that Feed-in Tariff or Net Metering will not apply to solar heating systems. However, there may be some other incentives available that will subsidize the installation costs.

Solar hot water systems could also be an excellent choice for heating swimming pools.
They do have to be sized correctly; see reference 1 for more details.

Maintenance Issues

All solar heating systems require some degree of maintenance because of the piping that runs all over the house. The more complex the system the more maintenance it needs. However, even the simplest system will require occasional cleaning of pipes and water tanks. Stagnant water must be avoided at all costs as it can be breed all kinds of bacteria including legionella.

The solar collectors run the risk of reaching an unsafe high temperature when the flow control valves are shut-off. Hence, it is essential to keep these systems running continuously, or to shut them off completely in a very safe manner. This means you should remove the solar panels from the roof when they are not in use. Also, in cold climates, there is always the risk of pipe damage in any part of the system due to freezing.

Pumps, too, require maintenance. They need periodic lubrication and if they are not in use for any length of time, there could be all kinds of problems including locking-up of the bearings. If pumps are unused for a long period of time, there are always problems during start-up including, occasionally, motor burnout.

Just contrast solar hot water systems with solar photovoltaic panels. The photovoltaics can function for years without any maintenance, as they use no moving parts at all.

8.3 Wind Power

If you live in a remote area and have plenty of land around your home, installing a windmill might be a viable option for you. At the very least, you should live on a one-acre lot but preferably much, much more. Also, you have to ensure that there are no ordinances that prohibit the installation of a windmill in your area. Finally, you have to make sure there is enough wind available at your site to power a windmill.

In general, urban areas are not suitable for generation of wind power. Even if there is sufficient wind, there are generally too many obstructions. Wind generators also create some noise that may pose a problem to others living in the area.

However, technology advances very rapidly and what is true today will definitely be false in the near future. Conventional wind generators use a horizontal axis, with the blades in a vertical plane. However, some recent designs use a vertical axis, with horizontal blades and these designs are much quieter; they are slowly finding their way into urban communities. Best Buy is currently installing such a system in Minneapolis and once the trials are over, we might see widespread use of these devices in Best Buy stores throughout North America.

So what does it take to make wind power a feasible option?

The very first requirement is availability of adequate wind force. According to the American

Wind Energy Association, you need an average annual wind speed of at least 9 miles per hour. Since we are talking averages, the actual wind speed does not have to be 9 MPH year-round. Also, wind turbines are mounted typically at a height of 60-120 feet above ground level. At these heights, the wind flow is much more.

In general, the areas with the best wind resources in North America are in the coastal areas, on mountain ridges or around the great lakes. The central plains also offer good sites for wind energy generation.

Information about wind resources is available on many web sites including:

www.awea.org

For Canada, see the web site:

http://www.canwea.ca/index_e.php

Some websites even have built-in tools where you can enter the location of your site and get an on-line assessment of the wind energy potential for your area. For example, this tool is designed for assessing wind energy potential at your site in Canada;

http://www.smallwindenergy.ca/calculator/home.php

Selection of Wind Turbines

Selecting a wind turbine for your residential

renewable energy project is a tad more complicated than selecting, say, a solar photovoltaic system. For starters, the method of test is not as standardized as is the case for photovoltaics.

Different manufacturers use different test conditions; there is no one standard for wind velocity at which the tests are performed. Hence one manufacturer may claim an output of 1000 watts at a wind speed of 12 miles per hour. Another may report an output of 1000 watts at 9 miles per hour. This does make comparisons between manufacturers a little difficult.

Again, the power output is not the only parameter to be considered – it is not even the most important because, in an actual application, the actual power generated by a wind turbine will also depend on the swept area.

This is simply the area of the circle described by the rotors as they move. The larger this area, the more wind the turbine will catch and this have a direct impact on the power that is generated.

Yet another variable is the height of the wind turbine tower. If the tower is a little bit higher, the wind turbine will experience a higher wind velocity and generate more output. The height is really very important, because power output varies as the cube of the wind velocity.

The windmill tower is an expensive component of the wind generation system. So, you have a choice between a bigger tower or a wind turbine with a bigger capacity. You have to work the best choice between these two components to see which will give you the best returns on your investment. If you use a wind turbine that generates DC, an inverter is also required.

Towers come in various designs. There are rack type towers that are really a rigid lattice type metallic structure that carries the weight of the wind turbine. Some of these are shipped as a single unit, while others come in sections so there is some assembly required. Most designs require a solid concrete foundation.

Then there are pole type wind towers that have the wind turbine mounted near the top. Again some assembly is required and a solid concrete foundation is also needed.

Most towers also need special equipment for installation, such as cranes especially in the larger sizes.

Maintenance is a big issue with wind turbines. Every wind turbine needs periodic lubrication; sometime the mechanical parts such as bearings and the rotor blades wear out and need to be replaced. Even minor maintenance work could require climbing to the top of the tower; it is not a job for the faint hearted. Just remember – wind turbines are often exposed to the worst weather you can think off – storms, heavy rain, sleet and snow.

Wind turbines cost $1.5-2.5/watt, according to *The Homeowner's Guide to Renewal Energy* 2006. In addition, the windmill tower is another expensive piece of equipment. You also need some electrical hardware such as an inverter, disconnects and a smart meter. If you add up all the costs, a 1 KW windmill would be about $14,700.00, according the same source. A 10KW system would cost $52,117.00

Hence, the price of a windmill installation is in the range of $5.2 to $15 per watt. There is a definite benefit to installing a larger system.

8.4 Water Power

If you have a natural source of water on your property, you should consider using a micro-hydroelectric generator for electricity. These systems work the same as the hydroelectric plants, but on a much smaller scale.

There are essentially two types of micro-hydroelectric systems. The first is installed at the base of a waterfall. The water flow drives a rotor or paddle wheel that generates electricity.

The second type is installed in a stream of water. You make a small dam that collects the water and the head of water is used to drive a small paddle wheel to generate electricity.

The micro-hydroelectric systems come in several flavours. You could have an AC system to generate power that runs appliance in your house, or, theoretically, provides power for the utility grid. Remember, the grid will accept only high quality power that is at exactly the right voltage, frequency and phase.

You could also have a DC system; in this case you will need an inverter to convert the power to AC, suitable for use in a power grid.

When sizing a micro-hydroelectric system, there are essentially two parameters to look at: the available water pressure head and the available flow rate. If you are a mechanical engineer you probably know these terms, otherwise you have to figure out what they really mean.

Pressure head

This is an engineering term for the pressure created by the height of water available to drive the micro-hydro-electric system, expressed in feet or metres. For example, a waterfall that is 10 meters high will have a pressure head of 10 metres.

Water velocity

This defines the velocity of the water at the point where the micro-hydroelectric unit is installed, expressed in units such as feet/minute or metres/sec.

Together, the pressure head and water velocity define how much energy is available for the micro-hydroelectric system. However, measuring these parameters with any degree of accuracy is an exercise in itself requiring, in most cases, professional expertise.

So, if you are considering a micro-hydroelectric system, make sure you call in a professional to do a site survey, take measurements as needed, and select a system that is appropriate for your site.

Micro-hydroelectric systems also require maintenance as they use quite a few mechanical components. Periodic maintenance is required for bearings, motors and the turbines, since most of the components are exposed to the atmosphere there may also be problems with pipes freezing up during the winter. If you like a maintenance-free system, then a micro-hydroelectric system is not the right choice for you.

Chapter 9: The Future of Renewal Energy

As conventional energy resources became increasingly scarce, it does not take rocket science to figure out that we will depend much more on renewable energy in the future. We all know that fossil fuel supplies are limited and they are being used up very quickly by oil-hungry world economies.

Oil prices are rising steadily; there may be occasional dips in the price, but, overall, the price just keeps going up. Electricity prices have been steadier, at least in North America, but there are subtle changes happening in the electricity market place.

Just one decade ago, the utility companies encouraged customers to consume more. Electricity was just a product to be sold in the market place; if more product was sold, there would be bigger profits for the sellers. Energy conservation was not on the utility companies' radar, as this concept was the very opposite of their own mantra:

"Sell more, produce more".

This mantra was popular until very recently and the use of renewable energy was way down the priority list for energy producers.

Today, utility companies all over North America

have taken to energy conservation; most of these companies offer rebates to customers for using energy efficient appliances. In Ontario, for example, the local utility company is currently offering programmable thermostats free of cost to its customers, to encourage energy savings. The company will even install the thermostat for free.

Such programs would be unheard of just a decade or two back. So it does appear that energy producers are changing their tune, to a large extent due to pressure from the general public and from government regulators.

That said, it must be admitted that the contribution of renewable sources to the overall energy production remains very small. In the US, coal-based power plants still produce the bulk of the energy, with a much smaller amount coming from nuclear power, natural gas and hydroelectric power. In Canada, hydroelectric power has a larger share but in both countries, renewable energy still accounts for a very small percentage of the total energy produced.

However, almost every form of conventional energy has serious problems associated with it. Let us discuss some of these issues before getting back to renewal energy.

Coal and Fossil fuels

Coal-based power plants are still responsible for the bulk of electricity production in most parts of the world. Some countries use other fossil fuels such as diesel and fuel oil but the supply of all of these fuels is limited. Fossil fuels are also responsible for much of the greenhouse gas emissions that many hold responsible for global warming.

Whether you agree or disagree with man-made global warming, the fact remains that use of fossil fuels in any form cannot, really, be good for the environment. With supplies dwindling around the world, we keep using lower grades of fossil fuels that are even worse for the environment.

Hydroelectric power

Hydroelectric power is a form renewable energy and it is a fairly clean source. It does, however, have some issues. Hydroelectric power generation is on the decline in many parts of the world as river systems keep drying up. Is this due to global warming? No one knows for sure, but that is another debate.

Luckily, Canada is relatively immune from dwindling water supplies as it still holds about one-fourth of the world's water resources. However, the effects are being felt rather sharply in the USA where there are many hydroelectric plants are being decommissioned.

There has also been much opposition to large-scale hydroelectric projects that often cause environmental damage. Sometimes, the ecology of entire regions is disturbed due to flooding caused by dams. As a result, hydroelectric power generation is no longer a growth industry in most parts of the world.

Nuclear Energy

Nuclear plants are very efficient at producing electricity, requiring fairly small quantities of fuel as compared to other sources of conventional energy. In recent times, there is a renewal of interest in nuclear energy as it has been touted as environmentally safe with no green house gas emissions. However, the long-term waste disposal problems simply cannot be brushed under the carpet forever –or buried under the ground, as some would like.

Proponents of nuclear energy claim that the waste disposal methods are very safe and this may well be true. However, the nuclear waste will not disintegrate for thousands of years because radioactive decay is a very slow process. Not only that, radioactive decays leads to the creation of other radioactive material that can remain in circulation for a very long time.

Also, North America is running out of disposal sites for radioactive waste.

The last disposal site under consideration by the US government was Yucca Mountain in Nevada in the middle of a desert. The site has some advantages due to its location. The amount of rainfall is very small so that there is very little groundwater in the area; this reduces risk of water contamination. The area is thinly populated and it is already owned by the military.

This is, however, an earthquake-prone area and it was recently discovered that the potential nuclear waste site is close to a fault line. The mountain, itself, was created by volcanic activity so it is not really a suitable repository for nuclear wastes.

So unless we want future generations to live in a highly polluted world full of nuclear waste, the only long-term solution to the world's environmental problems is to rely more on renewable energy. The faster we can make the switch to renewables, the better off we will be.

The limitations of conventional energy production lead to only one logical conclusion: we must find ways to accelerate the development of renewable energy. Like any other new industry, renewable energy production requires some incentives before it can stand on its own competitive feet.

Hence, a big part of the solution lies in developing more effective incentive programs for renewable energy growth. There are a number of policy options to consider:

Option 1: Offer no incentives

Under this option, no incentives would be for renewable energy programs, letting the market take care of itself. According to this school of thought, renewable energy projects will be implemented only when they become more cost-competitive.

The problem with this approach is that it pre-supposes a perfect free- market economy which does not really exist. Many people believe we live in a perfect free-market economy in North America. The reality is very different; we actually live in a lobby-driven free market economy. Lobby groups with the most powerful voice get the most benefits from the government. If there were no benefits to be had, there would not be any lobby groups.

Conventional energy companies have already enjoyed huge incentives at taxpayer expense. When the power industry was in its fledgling state, it made perfect sense to give it government support. Massive government subsidies helped set up the earliest hydroelectric and coal-based power plants throughout North America. The approach may well have worked for North America still enjoys some of the lowest utility rates in the world.

However, the "do-nothing" approach would be a disaster for renewable energy growth, because the industry is still too young to take off on its own. Renewable energy projects are not yet cost-competitive but with increased production of components at lower prices due to more volume, we are slowly getting there.

Option 2: Buy renewable energy at market price

Under this option, renewable energy producers are allowed to connect to the power grid but they are only paid at market rates. This system is already in use all over North America as Net Metering. Almost every US state and many parts of North America offer this. However, it has hardly resulted in a large-scale growth in renewable energy as compared to, say, Europe

Option 3: Offer incentives towards capital costs of renewable energy production

This approach has been tried with some degree of success in North America. The money, invariably, comes from the taxpayer in one form or another. Government subsidies helped create a wind power industry in California starting from almost nothing. These subsidies helped California become the world leader in wind energy production during the 1980s. Over the years, however, there has been a gradual slow down of government funding for renewable energy programs in California and the baton has now passed on to Germany which has more advanced incentive programs.

Government subsidies also helped rapid growth of wind energy production in upstate New York. Windmills have sprouted all over the countryside, with energy development companies signing up long term leases in remote farmland.

Government grants and subsidies can help get renewable energy projects off the ground very quickly but there are some problems. The source of funding can dry up any time as it is far too dependent on the political climate of the time. When a new political party comes into office, it is always very tempting to cut funding for programs initiated by the previous administration.

Also, large projects enjoy the economy of scale but they can lead to environmental problems. Large solar photovoltaic facilities take away productive farmland; wind farms create noise pollution and they can also be harmful to bird life in the area.

Smaller projects are less disruptive to the environment and blend in more easily with the surrounding landscape. So an incentive program geared towards small projects will be much more beneficial in the long run.

Option 4: Provide tax breaks for renewable energy generation

This approach has been popular in North America but most of the breaks help large companies that pay more tax. To create a real spurt in renewal energy production, there has to be greater involvement of a number of smaller players

Option 5: Impose energy taxes

This idea has been floated as a "carbon tax"; the objective, it appears, is to collect taxes from the producers or consumers of conventional energy and pass on the funds to renewable energy producers. This is a slippery slope; it is much more likely that the tax collectors will find other uses for the money.

Option 6: Expand Feed -In Tariff programs

Under this scheme, renewable energy producers are paid at higher than market rates for the electricity that they supply to the power grid. The utility recovers its money by distributing the costs over a large customer base. We have discussed this concept in great detail throughout the book.

From the policy point of view, FITs have many advantages. The major benefit is that this is a self-financing policy mechanism and there is no government subsidy involved. Hence this policy can easily survive political changes because a new administration will have no real incentive to cut a self-supporting program.

However, Feed-in Tariff have not always been successful – it all depends on how they are implemented and how much political will there is behind this policy. Many American states now offer FITS, but in many cases the tariffs are too low – as little as 12 cents/KWH in Kentucky. In a few cases, the tariff is kept marginally over the market rate for electricity supply. When the tariffs are kept too low, the market response is generally very poor.

On the other hand, FITs have been very successful in those European countries where they have been properly implemented. Some countries, like Germany, made a few false starts before getting the math right.

Ontario now offers a maximum FIT of 80 cents/KWh, one of the highest rates in the world. This promises to be a very successful program if the will to succeed carries over to successive administrations.

From this discussion, it appears that the most successful options would be:

Option 3: Provide incentive towards capital costs of renewable energy projects.

Option 4: Provide more tax breaks for renewal energy producers.

Option 6: Expand Feed -in Tariff programs.

Option 3 is, essentially, taxpayer funded and it has produced good results.

Option 4 has also been successful but it does tend to favour only large producers of renewable energy. Again, it requires government funding and requires sustained political will for successful implementation.

Option 6 is funded largely by the electricity consumers themselves. It has produced very successful results, especially outside North America. There have also been a few failures, whenever the program has not been set-up correctly.

So what is the best formula for success in the years to come?

Judging from past results, it seems to be a proper mix of capital cost incentives, tax breaks and a Feed-in Tariff program, taking the best features from each option.

Right now, there are simply not enough incentives provided towards the capital costs of renewable energy projects. This area needs to be beefed up considerably, in a way that will help both small and large producers of renewable energy.

More tax breaks should also be provided for development of renewable energy, to both small and large producers. This may require involvement of several government agencies, so it is a little harder to implement.

The Feed-in Tariff programs also need a tune-up.

Right now, Ontario has one of the better programs in North America but there are still areas for improvement.

1. The tariff for wind energy projects is a bit low at 15cents/KWh. It is definitely not enough to support small wind energy projects.
2. The requirement for domestic content reduces competition. It promotes the growth of local industry but it also encourages protectionism that invariably pushes up the costs.
3. The overall tariff structure needs continuous refinement as market conditions change.

Also, the Feed-in Tariff program must be used more widely North America; it has been adopted, so far, by only a handful of states and provinces. These numbers will, no doubt, grow as more policy makers realize the benefits of this approach.

There is a fundamental difference between the way incentive programs have been set up in North America and in Europe. In North America, legislation for incentive programs is at the provincial, state level or even the municipal level. This leads to wide disparities between the way different parts of North America implement this program; there is no coherent policy.

Europe, on the other hand, has introduced country-wide legislation creating a much better climate for success. North America needs to adopt a similar model to ensure widespread acceptance of the incentive programs.

A famous man once said:

"Build a better mousetrap and the world will beat a path to your door".

Producers of renewable energy might well say:

"Build a better incentive program and we will come to your door".

Chapter10: Useful Resources

This section lists additional sources of information that we have found useful; many of these are referenced in the pages of this book. There are thousands of web sites relating to renewable energy; we have picked a few and listed them by topic to help you with your renewable energy project.

A listing in this section does not, in any way, constitute an endorsement of the products, services or information offered by these web sites. We also make no guarantee, stated or implied, about the accuracy of the contents of these web sites.

Books and Magazines

Craig Morris
Energy Switch: Proven Solutions for a Renewable Future
New Society Publishers, 2006

Dan Chiras
The Homeowner's Guide to Renewable Energy
New Society Publishers, 2006

Energy
Elsevier Science Ltd.

Home Power
www.homepower.com

Photon
www.photon-magazine.com

Solar Energy International
Photovoltaics Design & Installation Manual
New Society Publishers, 2004

Web-sites

<u>Energy Savings Calculator</u>

http://rredc.nrel.gov/solar/calculators/PVWATTS/version1/International/pvwattsv1_intl.cgi

<u>Feed-In- Tariffs</u>

http://www.powerauthority.on.ca/

<u>General</u>

http://www.homepower.com/home/

<u>Incentive Programs</u>

http://www.dsireusa.org/
http://www.powerauthority.on.ca/

<u>Insolation Data</u>

https://glfc.cfsnet.nfis.org/mapserver/pv/municip.php?n=1408&lang=e
https://glfc.cfsnet.nfis.org/mapserver/pv/municip.php?n=1408&lang=e
http://www.solar4power.com/solar-power-insolation.html

Inverters

http://www.beyondoilsolar.com/inverters.htm
http://www.affordable-solar.com/xantrex-gt-28-inverter.grid.intertie.htm

Renewable Energy Analysis

http://www.retscreen.net/ang/version4.php

Renewable energy photographs

National Renewal Energy Laboratory
http://www.nrel.gov/data/pix/searchpix.php

Solar Panels

http://www.mrsolar.com/#
http://www.canadian-solar.com/en/products/regular-modules/index.html
http://www.realgoods.com/category/solar+power/solar+panels.do

Solar Panel Costs

http://www.ecobusinesslinks.com/solar_panels.htm
http://www.solarbuzz.com/Moduleprices.htm

Solar Panel Installation

http://www.solarpanelinfo.com/solar-panels/accessories/mounts/

http://www.prlog.org/10282272-solar-panels-roof-how-to-install-solar-panel-on-your-roof.html http://www.canadian-solar.com/en/corporate/about-us/index.html

Solar Panel Systems and Kits

http://www.wholesalesolar.com/complete-systems.html

http://www.affordable-solar.com

Chapter 11: Glossary of Terms

Advanced Renewable Tariffs: See Feed-in Tariffs

Ampere: Unit of electrical current

Ampacity: Current carrying capacity of a conductor

Array: A number of photovoltaic panels connected together

Avoided cost: A calculation by the utility company of the costs it avoids by not having to produce a certain amount of renewable energy

Azimuth: Angle between true south and a point directly below the sun; measured in degrees east or west of true south, in the northern hemisphere

Bypass diode: A device used to protect solar cells. It is connected across one or more cells such that the current will bypass the cell that is malfunctioning.

Conversion efficiency: The efficiency with which a photovoltaic device converts sunlight to electricity. Typically, a commercial photovoltaic array has a conversion efficiency of 14-20%.

Crystalline silicon: A type of silicon used in photovoltaic application; it is either a single crystal or polycrystalline i.e. a number of crystals joined together.

Direct insolation: Direct sunlight falling on a device.

Electrical grid: An integrated system of electricity distribution over a large area. Also known as power grid, utility grid.

Electricity Feed Law: See Feed-in Tariff

Feed-in Tariff: The tariff, or rate, at the utility which company pays a renewable energy producer connected to the grid. Also referred to as Electricity Feed Law, Advanced Renewable Tariffs, Production Incentives, Renewable Energy Payments.

Gigawatt: One billion watts.

Grid: See electrical grid

Grid-connected: A renewable energy system that is connected to the grid.

Grid-inter active: same as grid-connected.

Grid-intertie: same as grid-connected.

Hybrid system: A system using more than one form of renewable energy.

Insolation: The amount of sunlight falling at a location. Expressed in units such watts/sq.metres, KW/sq.metre.

Inverter: A device for converting DC into AC.

Junction box: An electrical enclosure for making proper electrical connections.

Kilowatt: One thousand watts, a measure of power

KWh: Kilowatt- hour; equals power of one kilowatt flowing for one hour

Megawatt: One million watts; 1000 kilowatts.

Module: A single assembly of photovoltaic cells

NEC: National Electrical Code; widely used in the USA. Canadian electrical codes are often modelled after NEC.

Ohm: unit of electrical resistance

Orientation: Placement of a device or system according to the compass directions.

Panel: A set of modules; sometimes used interchangeably with the term Module.

Peak sun hours: The number of hours when insolation averages 1000 watts/sq.metres

Power factor: An electrical term that describes the quality of power; the ratio of the average power to the apparent volt-amperes

Production Incentives: See Feed-in Tariff

Renewable Energy Payments: See Feed-in Tariff

Semi-conductor: A material that has limited capacity for conducting electricity.

Solar noon: The moment that divides the daylight hours for a location exactly in half.

Tilt angle: Angle of inclination of a photovoltaic module or array as measured in degrees from the horizontal.

Tracking system: A system that follows the path of the sun; maybe single-axis or a multi-axis system.

Volt: A measure of the force or push given to electrons in an electrical circuit.

Wafer: A thin sheet of photovoltaic material.

Watt: Unit of electrical power

Watt-hour: The energy that equals one watt used in one hour.

Chapter 12: List of Abbreviations

AC   Alternating Current

CSA   Canadian Standards Agency

DC   Direct Current

EPBT   Energy Pay Back Time

ESA   Electrical Safety Association

IESO   Independent Electricity System
Operator

FIT   Feed-in Tariff

NEC   National Electrical Code

NREL National Renewable Energy Laboratory

OEB   Ontario Energy Board

OPA   Ontario Power Authority

PV   Photovoltaic

RESOP   Renewable Energy Standard Offer
Program

Quick Index

For many readers, the Index is the most useful part of a book as it allows you to find the information that you need very quickly. In this book, we introduce the Quick Index that makes navigation even faster, by eliminating detailed references.

Advanced Renewable Tariffs	Ch.2
Approval process	Ch.6
Arrays	Ch 5, 5.3
Bill of Materials	Ch.5, 5.11
Building permit	Ch.6, 6.2
Declination	Ch.5, 5.2
Design phase	Ch.5
Disconnect switch	Ch5, 5.8
Domestic content	Ch 4, 4.3
Electrical Safety Authority	Ch.6, 6.4
Energy marketplace	Ch.3, 3.1
Feed-in Tariff	Ch.2, 2.1-2.8
Home resale value	Ch4, 4.3
Hydroelectric power	Ch 8, 8.4
Hydro Ottawa	Ch.3, 3.2
Insolation	Ch.5, 5.3
Insurance	Ch.6, 6.1
Installation	Ch.7
Incentives	Ch.2, Ch.9
Inverters	Ch.5, 5.7
Laws & regulations	Ch.4, 4.4;
Modules	Ch.5, 5.2
Myths, renewal energy	Ch.1, 1.3
National Electric Code	Ch.5, 5.9
Net Metering	Ch.1; Ch.2, 2.8

Ontario content	Ch.4,	4.3
Ontario Power Authority	Ch.6,	6.3
Ordering the equipment	Ch7,	7.1
Overcurrent protection	Ch.5	
Panel mounting	Ch.5,	5.7
Panel sizing	Ch.5,	5.5
Panel weight	Ch.4,	4.8
Photovoltaics	Ch.1, Ch.2,Ch.5	
Planning, solar electric project	Ch.4	
Rate of return	Ch.4,	4.9
RESOP	Ch.2,	2.6
Return on investment	Ch.4,	4.9
Simple payback	Ch.4,	4.9
Solar cells	Ch.5,	5.3
Solar heating	Ch.8,	8.2
Solar pv kits	Ch.5,	5.14
Testing	Ch.7,	7.2
Utility bill	Ch.3,	3.2
Water power	Ch.8,	8.4
Wind mills	Ch.8,	8.3
Wind power	Ch.8,	8.3
Wiring	Ch.5,	5.9

www.ingramcontent.com/pod-product-compliance
Lightning Source LLC
Chambersburg PA
CBHW071425170526
45165CB00001B/397